Plotto Genie For Pulp Fiction and Romantic Dramas

Escape Writer's Block and Generate Original Content Structure in Minutes

Using the Only 31 Basic Dramatic Situations Common To All Fiction Stories

(Derived from the original "The Plot Genie Index")

by **Wycliffe A. Hill**

Editor Notes:

These pages (not including the supplement) are a facsimile reproduction of the original text.

References to the use of a "Plot Genie" are for a random number generator that produces a result between 1 and 180. Many online versions are available. A spreadsheet may also generate random numbers with a cell-formula [=(RAND()*179)+1].

The original device apparently had a single big wheel numbered from 0 to 180 and was spun three times to produce a random number.

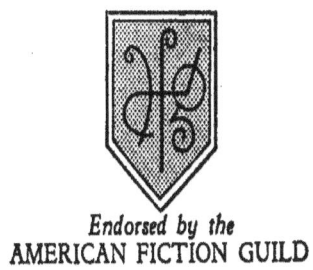

Endorsed by the
AMERICAN FICTION GUILD

DISTRIBUTED BY

The Gagnon Company

Hollywood, California

A Word From the Publisher

It is with a considerable degree of pride and satisfaction that I present this work to the literary fraternity. For a long time I have felt that there should be some practical and simple method designed which would not only be of assistance to literary students in the matter of plot building, but would be equally valuable to professional writers as a means of enabling them to quickly apply their creative powers when necessary. Therefore, when the author and inventor of the Genie system submitted his idea of a "Plot Genie" to me, I was immediately interested.

Further gratification was experienced by me when immediately after the publication of the first edition we began to receive enthusiastic letters of commendation and appreciation from many noted literary authorities, and I wish to thank them for the very helpful and worth while suggestions which have been made for the improvement of the work.

I sincerely share the opinion of other publishers who have expressed themselves as believing that this invention of the Plot Genie will have a definite bearing on the character of story plots around which much of our future fiction and drama will be built, to the end that stories in general will be improved in merit because they will be better plotted. I further feel that such a scientific system as is applied to the building of dramatic plots with this method is distinctly in line with the modern trend in all things toward efficiency and economy of effort.

Sincerely,

ERNEST E. GAGNON,
Publisher.

INDEX

LISTS

General Formula

for all types of stories and easily adaptable

to the love story melodrama

OPERATIONS   PLOT ELEMENT

(1)—(3 turns of the disc) supplies LOCALE or ATMOSPHERE

(2)—   "   "   "   FIRST CHARACTER

(3)—   "   "   "   THE BELOVED

(4)—   "   "   "   A PROBLEM

(5)—   "   "   "   OBSTACLE TO LOVE

(6)—   "   "   "   COMPLICATION

(7)—   "   "   "   PREDICAMENT

(8)—   "   "   "   THE CRISIS

(9)—   "   "   "   CLIMAX

IMPORTANT! Read instructions on the following pages very carefully before attempting to build a plot with the aid of the Genie.

Introduction

The Plot Genie, or "Plot Robot" as it has been publicized internationally by newspapers and magazines, is the result of sixteen years of effort to perfect a formula, and a means of its application which would enable student writers to inject plots into their stories. It has come from a process of evolution and is not an over-night creation devised as something to sell.

Sixteen years ago I was started on a rampant search in an effort to track the thing called "Plot" to its lair when the famous motion picture director and producer, Cecil B. De Mille, rejected one of my pet stories with the kindly criticism that "although an interesting narrative, it contains no dramatic plot."

Appealing to half a dozen celebrated motion picture dramatists of that time for an explanation of the difference between narrative and plot, brought me as many replies, which, although illuminating, were not satisfactory to me. It was about the same time I first learned that a book had been published which contained a list of all the basic dramatic situations—36 in number—and promptly purchased a copy. This was the beginning of an intensive study and analysis of dramatic plot building. After familiarizing myself with all the basic dramatic situations, I began to analyze books and motion picture plays and to observe how many, and just how and where the variations of these basic dramatic situations were used in their plots.

Some time later when able to form a satisfactory series of conclusions, I published the book, "Ten Million Photoplay Plots." This was about 1918 and was my first step in the direction of the Plot Genie.

In 1921 my book, "The Art of Dramatic Plot Building," was published. Credit must be given here to Will C. Wood (now Banking Commissioner for the State of California, who was at that time State Superintendent of Schools) for an innovation which the latter book contained. After reviewing the book "Ten Million Photoplay Plots," Mr. Wood called my attention to the fact that in order to successfully teach, one should follow the established rule of pedagogy, which is to provide definite assignments or tasks for the student, or examples for him to work out. This feature, which was introduced at his suggestion, made the book a very popular one with student writers.

Then again in 1925 I was employed by the Corona Typewriter Company to write the contents of "The Writers' Guide," which they advertised extensively the following year, giving away over one hundred and fifty thousand copies as a means of contacting writers and advertising the Corona typewriter.

This bit of history is given to lead up to the point which I wish to make here. It is this: In designing the Plot Robot-Genie my sole aim was to provide the new and inexperienced writer with a means of injecting a plot into his story, and I was the most surprised of all when professional writers began to write me enthusiastic letters describing the practical uses to which they were putting the device, in the plotting of their stories. In the first revision of the work I endeavored to bear in mind the requirements of the professional as well as those of the student writer.

It may or may not have been a mistake to give the name "Plot Robot" to the device when it was first put on the market, inasmuch as it is not really a robot. Although resulting in a tremendous amount of newspaper and magazine publicity, it also aroused considerable resentment and suspicion among the literati, some of whom were averse to the idea of a robot's doing intellectual work. Because of this feeling in regard to the name, it was decided to change it to "Plot Genie."

I believe that there is a specific formula for everything that exists. In other words, there are only a certain number of elements or ingredients introduced in the correct amount and proper order and acted upon by some kind of a catalyzing influence necessary to produce anything. It is a well-known fact that Nature produces beautiful designs in snowflakes accidentally, and that artists copy them. She also produces dramatic events in the same way and, after the news of their occurrence is circulated, writers who have to depend upon suggestion, seize upon such ideas for story plots.

The perfect story plot must be as carefully engineered as are the plans and specifications for any great structure. As is necessary in every formula, there are certain specific elements or ingredients which must be present and used in proper order and sequence. Therefore, the construction of a story plot is as simple as making and baking a pan of biscuits or as compounding a chemical mixture of any kind—when the proper formula is applied to the necessary ingredients.

ƒ

The ingredients necessary in a dramatic or story plot are: Places, People, and Dramatic Situations. The Plot Genie arbitrarily selects a locale and involves some character in a dramatic situation which is always productive of complications. It introduces a love affair and an obstacle to this affair. And then, it provides definite situations which furnish predicament, crisis, and climax—and you have a story plot.

In using this system of dramatic plot building it is important to remember that the process is as important as the formula. The mechanical part of the device is equally important with the index book because it arbitrarily, without choice to the writer, arranges a combination of characters, situations, and atmosphere which requires the application of a process of reasoning and the concentration of the creative imagination to justify the relationships of plot elements which at first glance seem totally foreign to one another. It thus induces trains of thought which may lead to veritable treasures in the way of story plot material. The mere perusal of the lists in the index book may or may not be of any particular benefit.

It is with pleasure that I hasten to acknowledge my obligation to a number of noted editors and authors who have voluntarily made numerous constructive suggestions based on their experiments with the Plot Genie and on a knowledge of story construction gained from long experience. Some of these suggestions have been adopted in this and other formulas for use with the Plot Genie.

Among these sincere friends are: Arthur Sullivant Hoffman, Eugene Cunningham, James P. Olson, Arthur M. Stone, Sewell Peasley Wright, Thomas Victor Gibson, Eugene V. Brewster, Treve Collins, Jack Smalley, Irving Willat, David Grew, Carl Coolidge, Captain James F. J. Archibald, Rebecca N. Porter, Isabel Stewart Way, A. L. Lewis, and G. A. Hartrampf.

However I am under the greatest obligation to the publisher, Ernest E. Gagnon, and it is with a feeling of sincere gratitude that I take this means of acknowledging that obligation. It was this publisher, with his broad-minded policy and far-sighted vision, backed up by the financial ability to guarantee the success of the undertaking, who made it possible for this entire work to be placed within the reach of all writers.

THE AUTHOR.

Only Thirty-one Basic Dramatic Situations on Which All Drama and Fiction Are Based

Past literary masters have for ages classified all the basic situations that can occur in Life, or the Drama, and the combinations of which form the basis of all fiction, under thirty-six heads.

Polti, the famous French writer, says that repeated efforts were made by Goethe, and others equally as learned, to vary from the original classification, but without success or satisfaction to themselves.

I contend that there are in reality only thirty-one basic dramatic situations. Two of these have never been included in the original thirty-six. In other words, I reject seven of the accepted list and add two new ones.

The Basic Dramatic Situations as Revised by This Author

MY CLASSIFICATION	ORIGINAL CLASSIFICATION
1—Rescue.	1—Rescue.
2—Misfortune.	2—Misfortune.
3—Supplication.	3—Loss of loved ones.
4—Obstacle to love.	4—Supplication.
5—Rivalry between unequals.	5—Obstacle to love.
6—Conflict between kinsmen.	6—Rivalry between unequals.
7—The enigma.	7—Rivalry between kinsmen.
8—To love an enemy.	8—Vengeance against kinsmen.
9—Sacrifice for an ideal.	9—Enmity between kinsmen.
10—Sacrifice for a loved one.	10—The enigma.
11—Fatal ambition.	11—To love an enemy.
12—Conflict between mortal and immortal.	12—Sacrifice for an ideal.

MY CLASSIFICATION	ORIGINAL CLASSIFICATION
13—Pursuit.	13—Sacrifice for a loved one.
14—Fatal indiscretion.	14—Fatal ambition.
15—Revolt.	15—Conflict between mortal and immortal.
16—Daring effort.	16—Pursuit.
17—Vengeance.	17—Effort to obtain.
18—Erroneous judgment.	18—Fatal indiscretion.
19—Sacrifice to passion.	19—Revolt.
20—Adultery.	20—Daring effort.
21—Criminal, or perverted love.	21—Vengeance.
22—Disaster.	22—Erroneous judgment.
23—Obligation to sacrifice a loved one.	23—Mistaken jealousy.
24—Madness.	24—Sacrifice to passion.
25—To learn of the dishonor of a loved one.	25—Adultery.
26—To slay a kinsman before recognition.	26—Murderous adultery.
27—Remorse.	27—Criminal love.
28—Recovery of loved one.	28—Involuntary criminal love.
29—Abduction.	29—Disaster.
30—Deception.	30—Obligation to sacrifice a loved one.
31—Blackmail.	31—Madness.
	32—To learn of the dishonor of a loved one.
	33—To slay a kinsman before recognition.
	34—Remorse.
	35—Recovery.
	36—Abduction.

The eight which I reclassify are: "Rivalry between kinsmen," "Vengeance against kinsmen," "Enmity between kinsmen," "Effort to obtain," "Mistaken jealousy," "Murderous adultery," "Involuntary criminal love," and "The loss of a loved one."

The first three I classify under one head, i. e., "Conflict between kinsmen." Little study is required to arrive at this conclusion. "Effort to obtain" is simply "Pursuit." There are only three things in existence that one could desire to obtain, and they are Revenge, Possession, and Relief—for self or loved one. There are only two ways of obtaining these, and they are Pursuit and Supplication.

"Mistaken jealousy" is nothing more or less than "Erroneous judgment" or an innocent suspected. "Murderous adultery" is adultery with murder, or a combination of several of the basic situations. There might be associated with adultery the following dramatic situations: "Sacrifice to Passion," "Pursuit," "Misfortune," "Supplication," "Conflict between kinsmen," "To learn of the dishonor of a loved one," "Abduction," or "To slay a kinsman before recognition." So it will be seen that "Murderous adultery" is a composite dramatic situation, in which the additional situations follow "Adultery."

"Involuntary criminal love" is merely a variation of "Criminal Love." In one, the guilty person is aware of the moral barrier existing, and in the other, he or she, is not. The fact remains that the love or infatuation is criminal just the same. "The loss of a loved one" is merely one of the variations of "Misfortune."

The two new ones? Ah! That is calculated to stir up a great deal of discussion or argument. However, I will stand by my guns in defending them.

"We find "Deception" and "Blackmail"—the two new dramatic situations —in every day real life drama.

In "Deception" confidence is outraged.

Here is an example: One week before Christmas a little tenement child sees a lovely vase in a shop window. She longs to buy it for her mother's Christmas gift. She enters the store and timidly inquires the price of the vase.

"More than you can pay," gruffly answers the shopkeeper.

The child holds out five pennies and says, "If I bring you five more, will you let me have it?"

The shopkeeper winks at his assistant and answers, "Sure."

All that week the child tries in every way to earn five pennies. Every time she passes the window she admires the lovely vase. Christmas Eve a kind neighbor gives the girl five pennies for running an errand. She is overjoyed and as she hurries along she visualizes her mother's delight on Christmas morning.

The vase is not in the window when she arrives at the store but she believes the storekeeper is keeping it for her. She enters and approaches the man.

"Here's the money," she says, handing him the five pennies. "Now may I have the vase?"

Her thin cheeks are flushed and her eyes are shining with happiness.

"The vase?" laughs the man. "Oh, I sold it an hour ago."

Even while the child is unaware of the deception that the shopkeeper is practicing on her, the reader senses it and the situation is dramatic, or it could not elicit sympathy or pity. To the man it is certainly dramatic, or it would not be possible for him to experience remorse.

"Blackmail" is the situation in which misfortune is threatened if a concession or sacrifice is not made. Angle one to the situation is the person who is threatened. Angle two is the relief from the predicament desired. The third is the blackmailer, or threatener, who stands in the way.

Basic Dramatic Situations Classified

From a study of the basic dramatic situations we find that there are some which provide PROBLEMS. Others can be more definitely classified under OBSTACLES TO LOVE; while a third group provides material for all manner of COMPLICATIONS and PREDICAMENTS, which are problems intensified or complicated. Following these are two other classifications. One of these is a situation which provides a CRISIS—or a still more serious and complicated problem. The other group contains the climactic conditions, or those which provide the CLIMAX in the story. The latter may either completely solve the problem or open the way to its solution.

The following is a list of the basic dramatic situations classified under the six heads: (1) Problem, (2) Obstacle to love, (3) Complication, (4) Predicament, (5) Crisis, (6) Climax.

(1) Problem

Situation No. 3—SUPPLICATION, or any situation in which some one pleads or begs for anything.

Situation No. 7—THE ENIGMA, or where there is a problem mystery which must be solved.

Situation No. 15—REVOLT, or where there is rebellion, uprising, or general revolt.

Situation No. 13—PURSUIT, or any situation in which an effort is made to accomplish anything where it is necessary to encounter obstacles.

Situation No. 17—VENGEANCE, or any situation in which a person seeks to avenge himself, loved one, society, country, religion, sect, or anything else against anything or anyone.

Situation No. 16—DARING EFFORT, or any situation in which someone is obliged to dare danger in order to accomplish anything.

(2) Obstacle to Love

Situation No. 8—TO LOVE AN ENEMY, or any situation in which it develops that a beloved one is an enemy.

Situation No. 2—MISFORTUNE, in which a lover or beloved one is handicapped physically, socially, mentally, or financially.

Situation No. 5—RIVALRY BETWEEN UNEQUALS, or any situation in which one of two rivals is greatly handicapped.

Situation No. 9—SACRIFICE FOR AN IDEAL, or any situation in which duty or obligation to an ideal stands in the way of a love affair.

Situation No. 10—SACRIFICE FOR A LOVED ONE, or any situation in which duty or obligation to a loved one stands in the way of a love affair.

Situation No. 6—CONFLICT BETWEEN KINSMEN, or any situation in which a lover's union is opposed by members of his or her family.

Situation No. 7—THE ENIGMA, or any situation in which a lover is required by his beloved to solve a problem or mystery.

Situation No. 21—CRIMINAL LOVE, or any situation in which it develops that lovers are blood kin.

Situation No. 18—ERRONEOUS JUDGMENT, or any situation in which an innocent is suspected, a misunderstanding, or mistaken jealousy.

(3) Complication

Situation No. 5—RIVALRY BETWEEN UNEQUALS, or any situation in which a greatly handicapped or unfortunate person is a rival with a normal person.

Situation No. 6—CONFLICT BETWEEN KINSMEN, or any situation in which there is a rivalry or enmity between kinsmen, or in which one kinsman pursues another for revenge, position, or anything else.

Situation No. 11—FATAL AMBITION, or any situation in which the ambition of another character for power, fame, riches, or anything else threatens to endanger himself or others.

Situation No. 12—CONFLICT BETWEEN MORTAL AND IMMORTAL, or any situation in which there is a rivalry or enmity between an ordinary person and one who is supposed to be endowed with supernatural power.

Situation No. 14—FATAL INDISCRETION, or any situation in which the conduct of a foolhardy person threatens to endanger himself or another.

Situation No. 20—ADULTERY, or any situation in which an illicit love affair threatens to complicate matters.

Situation No. 27—REMORSE, or any situation in which grief over having committed a real or imaginary crime or offense threatens to establish complications.

Situation No. 30—DECEPTION, or any situation in which a character or person is deceived as to real value, identity, or danger of an object, thing, or situation.

(4) Predicament

Situation No. 9—SACRIFICE FOR AN IDEAL, or any situation in which honor, principle, or duty to God or country stands in the way of possession, relief, or revenge.

Situation No. 10—SACRIFICE FOR A LOVED ONE, or any situation in which duty to a loved one stands in the way of possession, relief, or revenge.

Situation No. 15—REVOLT, or any situation in which there is threatened a revolt, rebellion, mutiny or uprising.

Situation No. 18—ERRONEOUS JUDGMENT, or any situation in which an innocent person is accused or suspected of having committed a crime or offense voluntarily or otherwise.

Situation No. 19—SACRIFICE TO PASSION, or any situation in which the weakness of a character for some habit, passion, or mania threatens a predicament for himself or others.

Situation No. 24—MADNESS, or any situation in which the deranged mind of a character threatens to place himself or others in a predicament, or in which the mind of any character is threatened with derangement from insanity, hypnotism, torture, grief, drugs, or anything else.

Situation No. 29—ABDUCTION, or any situation in which a character is either abducted or kidnapped or seriously threatened with same.

Situation No. 31—BLACKMAIL, or any situation in which a character is threatened with physical, mental, social, or financial loss or injury unless a sacrifice or concession is made.

(5) Crisis

Situation No.   2—MISFORTUNE, or any situation in which serious injury, loss of life or health, loved one, fortune, sanity, possession, honor or good name is immediately threatened.

Situation No. 24—MADNESS, or any situation in which the conduct of a mentally deranged person threatens to bring disaster on himself or others, immediately.

Situation No. 11—FATAL AMBITION, or any situation in which the fatal ambition of a character for possession, relief or revenge, threatens to bring immediate disaster to himself or others.

Situation No. 14—FATAL INDISCRETION, or any situation in which the lack of judgment, or foolhardy conduct on the part of a character threatens to bring immediate disaster to himself or others.

Situation No. 15—REVOLT, or any situation in which there is immediately threatened a rebellion or serious uprising, strike, mutiny, or boycott.

Situation No. 22—DISASTER, or any situation in which a great catastrophe is immediately threatened, such as a flood, massacre, epidemic, or anything else of the kind.

Situation No. 25—TO LEARN OF THE DISHONOR OF A LOVED ONE, or any situation in which the dishonor or disgrace of a person is about to be brought upon his or her loved ones.

Situation No. 26—TO SLAY A KINSMAN BEFORE RECOGNITION, or any situation in which a character is about to slay any unrecognized kinsman or friend or about to refuse rescue to such a one whose identity is not known.

Situation No. 23—OBLIGATION TO SACRIFICE A LOVED ONE, or any situation in which it appears that one is obliged to make a sacrifice of a loved one.

(6) Climax

Situation No.   1—RESCUE, or any situation in which a character is rescued from peril or from impending misfortune of any kind.

Situation No. 17—VENGEANCE, or any situation in which a despised character or one who has committeed a crime or offense is punished.

Situation No. 28—RECOVERY OF A LOST LOVED ONE, or any situation in which a loved one who has been lost is restored.

Situation No. 9—SACRIFICE FOR AN IDEAL, or any situation in which a character sacrifices possession, relief, or revenge in order to satisfy honor, principle, duty to God, or country.

Situation No. 10—SACRIFICE FOR A LOVED ONE, or any situation in which a character sacrifices possession, relief, or revenge for the sake of a loved one.

Situation No. 24—MADNESS, or any situation in which a story ends with the loss of reason, memory, or mind, on the part of any character.

Situation No. 26—TO SLAY A KINSMAN BEFORE RECOGNITION, or any situation in which one who has been slain or refused a rescue, develops to have been an unrecognized kinsman.

Situation No. 15—REVOLT, or any situation in which a people revolt against injuries, tyranny, or oppression.

Dramatic Plot Building

The writer should bear in mind that all dramatic plots are composed of combinations of certain elements just as melody or tune is the result of a combination of various notes of the octave and their shadings or variations. It is all a matter of composition, just as is a beautiful picture.

In a dramatic plot there are two elements, i.e., people and dramatic situations. One is involved in the other. The story must always contain one or more problems which affect certain characters, and then the question of whether or not these problems will be solved, and how they are to be solved immediately, affords suspense and entertainment—necessities in a dramatic plot.

There are a number of ways in which a character may set about solving a problem which confronts himself or a loved one. He may use prayer, ruse, or strategy, force, threat, or barter. Resorting to these is likely to precipitate further conflict or bring about added complications which must be overcome. Therefore, the plot becomes more complex and the drama more intense.

One of the tricks of the trade is to introduce a surprise situation or development which quickly extricates the principal character from a serious predicament which appears unsolvable. Thus, a climax is brought about which paves the way for the happy ending. (We are considering now the melodramatic love story.)

One of the most common faults of the beginner is that of mistaking narrative for dramatic plot and thereby of submitting the former type of story when only the latter is desired.

A dramatic plot is the combination of a number of dramatic situations involving a number of characters. These situations must have a definite relationship to each other, and must intensify as they progress toward the climax. In other words, each dramatic situation in the plot must be the result of the preceding one and the cause of the one that follows, and they must lead to the climax, which is a combination of all the dramatic situations.

Nothing can be dramatic without conflict. There must be someone who wants something, and there must be an obstacle in the way of the thing desired. These three things:—The person who wants something; the thing that is wanted; and the obstacle in the way, form or comprise the dramatic situation in every plot. The dramatic situation is a part of the dramatic plot, or, as stated above, the dramatic plot is a composite of a number of correlated situations.

Every dramatic plot must introduce conflict, or a complication which means conflict between people or between people and circumstances. One of the principals may desire the love of another, riches, fame, pleasure, authority, relief, recognition, or revenge. There must be an obstacle in the way. The manner in which he goes about securing the object of desire; the increasing opposition of the obstacle, the positions of jeopardy that develop and are subsequently avoided—either purposely or accidentally—and the final scene in which the object of desire is either won or lost, constitute the plot.

A narrative is merely the description of a series of incidents, some of which may be dramatic, but which have no direct relation to each other. In other words, it is a rambling story in which there is no thread of suspense and which does not build up in intensity as the end is approached. For instance, the book, "Robinson Crusoe" is a very interesting narrative, but it would make a very uninteresting screen play since it is merely a relation of the varied experiences of a man in unusual surroundings. While conflict appears spasmodically it is not sustained throughout as is required in the dramatic plot.

As outlined above, there are thirty-one basic dramatic situations, and all plots must be composed of two or more of these basic situations. There is no other material in the world with which to build plots, but there is, nevertheless, an almost infinite number of variations of these situations. Furthermore, the combinations of situations can bring about almost innumerable variations of plot. In fact, there are as many variations possible in plot building as there are in melody-making from eight major notes.

Just as no two people look alike or possess the same kind of thumb print, so no two carefully constructed plots need be alike. Thus, it will be easy to understand how the Plot Genie can assist the author in creating new plots. With it, the novice and the expert alike can build dramatic plots as a mathematician juggles figures, and such a writer will be able in a short time to create enough plot material to keep him busy writing the rest of his life.

Rounding out the Plot

Having now considered the proposition of where and how to get plot material and that of building the framework, our next step is that of rounding out the plot. In other words, we are to consider the matter of technique.

It makes no difference how good a dramatic plot we have invented, if the story is not told or presented properly, it fails. We must go back over our plot and ask ourselves these questions: Is the plot logical?—Does it sustain interest throughout?—Are the characters human?—Is their motivation correct?—Does the plot introduce suspense and hold it until the end?—Have we worked up to a big climax?—Does the plot contain any blind alleys?—Are there any loose ends?—Any unexplained elements?—How about the introduction of pathos and heart interest?—Is there any comedy relief?—Can the reader foretell the climax?—Is the plot hackneyed?—Have we permitted an anti-climax? Let us now take up the study of these two elements.

Suspense and Climax

In every well developed story we have a number of sub-climaxes in addition to the real climax at or near the end of the story. Generally speaking, climax is the highest dramatic point to which a situation ascends, and then breaks. The real climax of a story or plot is the big situation which comes as a solution to the opening complication. It is the culmination of everything that has gone before in the plot.

Suspense and Climax go hand in hand. One cannot exist without the other. In other words, a climax must be preceded by suspense, otherwise it falls flat. And again, if suspense is present—a climax is bound to follow when the dramatic situation reaches the highest point to which it can go—and breaks. In the most strained and exciting situation, something must happen. Whatever happens is the climax. The terrible uncertainty as to what is going to happen is suspense.

Suspense is therefore the element of profound interest and uncertainty of the outcome which accompanies a dramatic plot or situation. The more intense the dramatic situation, the greater the suspense. In the average popular love story we have two threads of suspense running parallel throughout. One works up to a lesser climax, breaks and starts again immediately, as a situation affecting the life, liberty or happiness of the principal character. In other words, this is the thread which accompanies the progressive series of lesser climaxes that take place throughout the story.

The other, or main thread, is the one which begins with the opening complication, or dramatic situation, as soon as we get acquainted with the principal character in the story. It continues, unbroken, to the main climax near the end of the story which decides his fate.

As a rule, it is desirable to bring all the principal characters in the story as near together as possible for the final climax. If this is not done, an anti-climax is likely to result.

To avoid the anti-climax, develop the story to the exact point where the climax takes place,—and then STOP! Do not kill your climax with any further developments.

Here is a good example of an anti-climax which should be easily understood. Let us suppose that two young men with whom we are acquainted are both in love with the same girl. They are college athletes. Both are captains of football squads for their respective universities. There is a test game coming off. The girl thinks she loves them both, and has made up her mind that she will marry the one that wins. Fine! The game is a terrific battle throughout which we are kept in suspense. Perhaps we like one of the fellows better than we do the other. Maybe we have discovered that one of them has planned to "throw" the game. That heightens our interest and the suspense. Now, we are not only interested in seeing the other fellow win because he deserves to do so, but there are high stakes in sight. Again and again it looks as if the villain's side is going to win. The blacker it looks for our hero, the greater will be the suspense. Finally, the hero's side wins by a scratch. The girl rushes into his arms as he comes up exhausted. The villain looks on with hatred and disappointment. We are exultant! Here is our climax. It is great! If the story ends there we feel that we have been properly entertained.

But wait! Just as the girl throws her arms about our hero, a secret service man walks up and placing his hand on the boy's shoulder, announces that he has a warrant for his arrest! Here is the beginning that constitutes a decided anti-climax. The result is that the reader is disgusted. He wanted to read ONE story through to a satisfactory ending. He is not interested in and does not want to be bothered with another.

Motivation

The ultimate object of every story writer is to create an emotional reaction in the mind of his reader, and he should plan his story with this end in view.

It rests with him whether he shall make his reader laugh or weep, suffer or rejoice, as through the power of his artistry he is able to convey these emotions to his readers through the actions and speech of his characters.

Each action of each character produces a certain effect and the certainty with which this will arouse an emotional response in the reader is governed by the cause behind the effect. This cause and resulting effect in fiction and drama is known as motivation and the writer would do well to make a careful study of this element. Unless each effect is the result of a logical cause the actions of the characters in the story will not be convincing.

The art of motivation is not difficult to learn. It might be concisely defined as cause and effect—BECAUSE certain things happen they give rise to other action which creates a certain pre-conceived effect. It has been said that a writer first shows the reader that something may happen and then proceeds to have it happen.

Motivation intensifies drama for when the reader realizes the cause underlying the actions of a character, he will react more readily to the situations or predicaments in which that character finds himself.

If a story is properly motivated it will be convincing because it will have an atmosphere of logic and probability. This illusion of reality will make it seem a fragment of life itself rather than a creation of the author's imagination.

Blind Alleys

Blind alleys lead nowhere. They are just false scents which cause us to stray from the main path and not only lose valuable time, but fall behind the rest of the procession. That is exactly what happens when we open a blind alley in a story.

To open a blind alley in the story means to establish a false premise. It may be in the introduction of a character who for a time occupies the center of the stage and then drops out of the story. The reader is led to believe that such a character will play an important role, only to be disappointed by his disappearance.

Another form of a blind alley is a bit of action on the part of some of the characters which leads the reader to believe that some important development will follow as a consequence.

Straight Line Stories and Those Carrying Sub-Plots

A straight line story is one in which there is a single conflict. Someone desires something very much. The manner in which these obstacles offer increasing opposition—how the life, liberty, or happiness of the principal character is placed in jeopardy—and how the obstacle is finally overcome, constitutes a straight line story.

The complex plot is one in which a second conflict between the hero or heroine and outside forces—or a conflict which exists between two outside elements—is introduced. In other words, the straight line story embraces a single dramatic triangle, while the complex plot may introduce a double or multiple set of angles. As the writer can understand, more than one dramatic triangle is extremely difficult to handle so as to hold the attention of the audience or reader in a way that is not confusing.

Pathos—Heart Interest—Surprise

There should be touches of pathos and heart interest in every story—as well as the element of surprise. Pathos is that quality in the story which excites pity. It may be introduced with a bob-tailed puppy which has its leg broken. A rivalry between unequals, the supplication of an unfortunate, or the struggle of any being against overwhelming odds, is pathetic because it excites pity.

Heart interest is that responsive chord in the heart which is struck by witnessing an object or incident, the significance of which is brought home to us. A litter of pigs or puppies; a playful domestic pet; a canary; a mother's love for her infant; the portrayal of sweet innocence; or the tender affection of an old couple, are beautiful touches which add heart interest. In other words, it is the purer and nobler things in life, devoid of conflict or selfish desire which touch the tender chords of the human heart. The touches may be ever so delicate, yet they are the little high-lights which make the pictures perfect. A ragged newsboy leading a blind man across a traffic-jammed street will not fail to touch a tender chord in the most calloused heart. A study of the covers of the front pages of many of the popular magazines will reveal an example of the things which make for heart interest.

Example of Pathetic Situations

A man who has succeeded in mounting to fame with the assistance of a self-sacrificing and devoted wife—who has outstripped her socially, so to speak —becomes cold toward her, critically compares her manner of appearance with other younger and more beautiful women. The lines in her face—those dark rings under her eyes—and the rough texture of her skin—have all come as a result of the sacrifices she has made for him. Now he studies—and compares her with—other younger women who have suffered nothing—who know nothing of privation and sacrifice. Perhaps he is just thoughtless, but it hurts her. Although she remembers how she has stood by his side ‚when he had nothing—was nobody—still she makes another effort to "primp up"—to hide those lines of care—to smooth out those wrinkles, just to please him. He comes in and finds her hoping for a word of praise. He does not notice her, and talks of his professional accomplishments. Shyly she tries to attract his attention, but still he does not notice her. She groans inwardly and turns away! That is pathos.

Here is another situation which is full of pathos—one which occurs in "The Sign of the Rose," a well-known starring vehicle in which the late George Beban was featured all over the country. It was also produced on the screen.

A poor Italian, who has not been in America very long, comes home one night from a hard day's labor and finds that his only loved one on earth, his little girl, Rosie, has been run over and killed by an automobile. His extreme grief is pathetic. Later, he finds a youngster who has strayed from home, and his love for the departed Rosie is lavished upon the new-found child. Through circumstances, wholly accidental, it is made to appear that he has kidnapped the child. He is arrested, and learns that the man who has had him arrested is the same one whose big automobile ran over and killed his little Rosie. He protests his innocence, but to no avail.

Here we have an extremely pathetic situation, which gives an opportunity for a good actor to display some wonderful work.

Dramatic Action Not to Be Confused With Physical Action

Dramatic action is one thing and physical action is another. Too many students confuse the two when the term "action" is used in the description of a plot. Dramatic action does not necessarily mean violent physical movement. It may picture an inward struggle that approaches the superhuman, yet there may be little physical movement.

Sometime ago I read a story in which the hero is captured by the enemy and subjected to torture. The enemy rigged up a stretching machine by fastening ropes to the hero's head and feet, which are connected with a windlass. The enemy then pulls the hero's body taut and demands that he disclose the whereabouts of certain valuable maps. As he refuses, the windlass is turned and the ropes tightened. Again he refuses to be a traitor to his country—even to save himself. Again and again the ropes are tightened, until the veins in his face stand out like whipcords. Here we have an illustration of intense dramatic action with very little physical motion, as the face of the hero and his agonized cries tell of the terrible physical torture that he is suffering.

Two men meet in the dark. One is a burglar and the other the intended victim. They cannot recognize one another, and a fight to the death results. When the victor strikes a match, he finds that the burglar is his own son. He remembers how he has driven the boy away from home for a trivial offense—forced him into starvation—and now he has killed him.

There is great dramatic action as the father contemplates the stiffening form of his own boy, and a remorse that is worse than hell itself takes possession of his soul. He cries out in mental agony—dramatic action of the most powerful kind—with practically no physical movement. There are several of the basic dramatic situations involved in this incident. It would be a useful exercise to pick them out.

Spectacle

Spectacle means spectacular events such as a collision between two loco-motives; a battle between armies; mobs in a riot; an earthquake, flood, etc.

Spectacle is valuable in a story only when it affects the fates of our principal characters. It has been said: "A circus may legitimately have sideshows, but the drama cannot." There is a danger in substituting spectacle for dramatic action. It may obliterate the finer mechanism of the drama with a realism that satiates, which makes everything that follows seem insipid. The entire plot may be lost in the wreckage of the spectacle.

Spectacle merely assaults the nerves, while true drama appeals to the heart. Romanticism and idealism may be completely overwhelmed by spectacle. The contributive elements to romance or idealism must be delicate, not spectacular. Even melodrama may be spoiled by too much spectacle. This is illustrated in such works as "The Hair-Raising Exploits of Dick the Diamond Robber," and some of the serial stories we see on the screen and read in the cheaper magazines.

The Dramatic Scale

The scale of dramatic entertainment may be said to run as follows:

    (1)   Romantic, or Ideal, Drama.
    (2)   Comedy Drama and Satire.
    (3)   Melodrama.
    (4)   Burlesque, Straight Comedy and Comedy Melodrama.
    (5)   Farce and Slapstick.

There is a decided difference between pure drama and melodrama, yet the dividing line is invisible. There is an overlapping of one into the other. Pronounced melodrama is pure drama exaggerated. We approach melodrama as soon as the dramatic action in our story assumes a sensational nature. The characterization of the principal characters in melodrama, both the good and the bad elements, are somewhat overdrawn. The hero and heroine are shown to be very, very good, while the actions of the opposing factions are extraordinarily violent. Murder, abductions, fights, robberies, and devilish plots have their place in melodrama. Here we have a purely physical conflict. In the drama of the romantic, or ideal type, we have more of a spiritual struggle.

In comedy drama, we have a pronounced element of comedy throughout the drama. There are serious or dramatic moments in comedy-drama, but none in straight comedy. Comedy may be injected into melodrama also, making it comedy-melodrama. Satire is witty censure, and a form of comedy-drama. Burlesque is an imitation of drama, done in ridicule. It is clownish, while satire is dignified. Slapstick comedy is melodrama exaggerated to the point where it becomes ridiculous.

Theme—Inspiration—Characterization

One of the most important factors to be considered in writing a story is the selection of a theme. There are many kinds of themes. Some are good and some are bad. Some depend for their popularity on their timeliness, or the existing public frame of mind. There are some themes that are always good, and still others which are at all times questionable, if not to be avoided altogether. Among those which are always good might be listed: self-sacrifice, mother love, patriotism, loyalty, faith, reward of merit, etc.

Among the themes which should be avoided are: the race question—or a story which has a tendency to arouse enmity and antagonism between the races; those which stimulate class hatred, or arouse the ire of one class or sect against the other. A story which casts reflection on any religion, as well as those which depend for their chief interest on the sex problem, are always questionable themes.

As stated before, some themes are popular at one time and not at another. For instance, during the World War, patriotism and militarism were rampant, and there was naturally a great demand for stories dealing with military and naval operations. Patriotism and War were chief themes. A short time after peace was declared these themes became very unpopular, and there was no market whatsoever for war stories. We then had a season in which stories dealing with spiritualism and psychic matters were very popular. This probably resulted from the fact that friends of those killed in the war wished to communicate with the spirits of the departed.

One motion picture producer succeeded in popularizing the divorce theme, and there followed a deluge of pictures dealing with the divorce and domestic problem. There have been many other themes, the popularity of which has gone in cycles. The author who is able to reach the market at the proper moment with a story carrying a timely theme is likely to realize high returns for his effort. On the other hand, he risks losing out completely should his story arrive too late. Hence, it is considered the best policy to write on such themes as are always good.

The treatment of any theme requires the delicate exercise of good judgment. While remaining passively impersonal himself, the author conveys powerful personalities to the characters whom he creates. He should therefore remain always on the side of justice, decency, and good citizenship. Embodied in the hero should be the figure of Justice, which shows no mercy to the wrong-doer, yet whose sympathies are always with that which is pure, noble and good. It is not necessary for the writer to be a prude or preacher. His work should inspire better things rather than to attempt to teach them.

Characterization

One of the most important elements in fiction, the drama, or the photo-drama is characterization. It is this vital picturization of life that distinguishes the work of a real artist from the dauber. A knowledge of plot construction must be mastered, but just as important is the study of characterization. As a matter of fact, many fiction writers have succeeded by and through their art of unusual and wonderful character drawing.

In fiction, it is possible to portray character both by description and action. The novelist may soar into starry heights in his eloquent description of a chosen character. With mere words he may paint his hero or heroine in dazzling fashion. In order to depict character, suitable action and dialogue must be given the principals in the story. Still, this action must not be such that it is irrelevant to the plot of the story. It must absolutely advance the story. In other words, it is not permissible to introduce action which is inconsequential to the plot in order to establish the individuality of the character.

To be a successful story writer one must be a student of human nature as well as of dramatic situations. Each character in the story has his traits. To a large extent these traits shape the actions which lead to the dramatic situations. One of the serious mistakes that may be made by the student is to write a character "out of character." If the leading man is supposed to be dignified, he must not be given a bit of business that makes him appear otherwise; or, if the villain is brutal, it would be a fatal mistake to have him perform a sympathetic act.

In characterization, it is not sufficient to merely say that a man is dignified, faithful, courageous, sympathetic, gallant or gentle. His actions and speech must demonstrate that he is such. Hence, it is of the utmost importance that the writer be ready to suggest a concrete example of deportment that will establish character. The action suggested, must *not* be of such nature that it is foreign to the story. Character may be established by a simple expression of the face, or by a well-chosen reply.

We establish the fact that a man is dignified if we say that he refused to smile when a silly joke was told; or, that he is firm when "he brought his fist down on the table with a bang and refused to listen any further." We understand that he is polite if he tips his hat to a lady, or stands with his head bared while talking to her. We show that he is courteous if he offers his seat in a car to a lady; or gallant, when he knocks down a man who is abusing her. If he keeps up an incessant tapping on the table with his pencil when he is being harangued, we know he is nervous; while if he leans back and blows a ringlet of smoke from his cigar, it is evident that he is cool and nonchalant. If he refuses employment to a girl whose fingernails are not properly manicured, we portray the fact that he is discriminating. Should the girl fall into a fit of weeping and cause him to revoke his decision, we conclude that he is compassionate. He then tells the girl why he decided against her, and we show that he is frank. The girl tells him her sorrows, and a tear forms in his eye, which tells that he is sympathetic. Later, when she makes a mistake and he reassures her and gives her another chance, he stamps himself as being patient.

Why So Many Authors Write Hackneyed Plots

Frequently we hear an egotistical person advance this argument: "Oh, I don't need anything to help me get ideas, my head is just full of plots."

The truth of the matter is that nine hundred and ninety-nine out of a thousand people who are trying to write stories either resort to the use of hackneyed and worn-out plot combinations, or have no real plots at all.

There is a reason for this, and it is a simple one. It is what I term the

ASSOCIATION OR CORRELATION OF IDEAS. Did you ever pause to wonder why all "Western" stories are alike? Or why all underworld stories are so similar in plot? Or why mystery stories all seemingly come from the same mold? And why there is in general such a similarity in types of stories that publishers are worrying themselves sick over the story problem?

Ideas That Hang Together

What I mean by "the association or correlation of ideas" which is the cause of so many hackneyed plots, may be illustrated in this way: To the average writer the mention of a "Western" story, which would naturally have a cattle ranch or a mining camp as a background, would immediately suggest, in case of the cattle ranch, cowboys, cattle rustling, and the pretty city maiden who is courted by the manly cowpuncher. In other words, these plot elements have been used so much in stories that they have become associated with one another to the extent that one automatically suggests the other. In the case of the mining camp story there is immediately suggested an old prospector with a beautiful daughter, a villain claim-jumper and a hero from the city. The association of these ideas has resulted in thousands of mining camp stories being written around some variation of this plot.

The mere mention of African diamond mines suggests to the average writer, handsome English army officers or American soldiers of fortune involved in a mystery connected with the smuggling of uncut precious stones and perhaps a battle with the natives, and a love affair with the captain's daughter. South Sea Islands suggest a beautiful, half-clad native girl and some globe-trotting, wealthy young American languishing under the spell of her beauty.

I could go on describing examples of the "association or correlation of ideas" which is responsible for the rut into which thousands of writers fall, and for the tens of thousands of hackneyed stories which they write, and then wonder why they do not sell. Any editor could tell you that there is such a rank similarity of ideas paraded across his desk daily that he is ready to throw up his hands in despair before he has read the first dozen manuscripts, and then when something that is really novel and refreshing does come along, he could almost throw his arms around the author.

Breaking Up The Old Associations

The "association of ideas" means nothing to the Plot Genie. The mention of a cattle ranch does not suggest a cowboy, much less a cattle rustler, to him. Nor does a mining camp suggest the prospector.

In glancing over six plot synopses which the Genie developed in thirty minutes, I find that it has placed a savage in a coliseum, a publisher on a farm, a hypnotist in a jungle, a baroness in a bowery, a chemist on the Amazon River, and an acrobat in the South Sea Islands.

Nevertheless, any one of these six plot structures could very easily be developed into a story for either novel or screen, and it would be "different," indeed.

The very fact that the Plot Genie is not handicapped by ideas which insist on sticking to one another, but that it is free to create any and all manner of combinations such as would be utterly impossible for the mind of any human being to do, explains why Genie story plots are not hackneyed ones. To sum it all up, the mind of the average author who prides himself on his imagination, and proudly declares that his mind is "teeming with plots," in reality has a brain storehouse which is all cluttered up with wreckage of second-hand story ideas.

The ideas which are selected by the Plot Genie from the immense storehouse in the index book for the construction of millions of new and novel plot combinations, come separately so that they may be fitted together into an absolutely new structure. In that manner, the old associations are broken up and unusual stories result.

I contend that the idea of an author moping around in a trance while he waits for a story-inspiration, is utterly absurd. Everything that ever did happen, that is taking place, or that will occur in this world, was, is, or will be nothing else than a combination of dramatic situation, character and background. The number of plot elements is known and limited. The nature and proportion of those which are used in the story formula, the order in which they are introduced, and the reaction which results from the mixture, is what provides an unlimited number of plots.

With the aid of the Plot Genie one does not have to wait for a rare flash of inspiration for a story. The Genie will provide a complete plot framework every five minutes, and I can show any author where it could have developed the plot structure of any story he ever wrote.

Furthermore, the Plot Genie will develop plot combinations faster than all the famous authors in the world combined, if they rely on the "muse" of inspiration.

How to Use the Plot Genie

In the very beginning I want to impress upon the mind of my reader that in using the Plot Genie to develop story plots, the process is as important as the formula. By this I mean that if one would succeed in the development of novel and refreshing plots and in experiencing a real stimulation of the creative imagination, he should not attempt to construct a plot by merely picking or choosing the various elements from the lists in the book. Neither should he substitute any element contained in the various lists for any one which is indicated by the Plot Genie disc—at least not until after the first plot structure is completed.

The point which I wish to make here is that if one is permitted to exercise his own choice in the selection of the nine ingredients from the list, he will subconsciously choose those which have an obvious relation to one another because they have been associated before, the result being that the plot constructed is hackneyed, or similar to many other stories which have been written and published or produced in the past. There is a special exception, however, which has been made in paragraph 8 in the following "Special Suggestions" for the benefit of those authors who are using the Plot Genie for the practical purpose of developing story material for special markets, rather than for practice in dramatic plot construction.

By its arbitrary selection of background, characters and dramatic situations for you, the Plot Genie will compel the creative imagination to be exercised in the blending of these ingredients. The Genie tells you what happens, and when you have figured out how it could happen that way, you have not only exercised your creative imagination, but you have actually developed a story plot. Also, you will discover that you have been stimulated to introduce angles that you would never have thought of in any other way.

Now, before we actually take up the Plot Genie and begin to build story plots, I want you, my collaborator, to carefully study the following special suggestions:

Special Suggestions

(1) Hold the cardboard Genie so that you do not buckle it or pinch the disc. It is best to hold it in the hollow of the left arm, grasping the top of it with the left hand.

(2) Observe that there are two lists each of male and female characters, the "Usual," and the "Unusual." With operation number 2 you obtain the lover for your story, taking it from one of the male lists, and operation number 3 supplies you with the beloved one from one of the female lists. It is a good plan to decide in advance whether you are going to use the "Usual" or the "Unusual" character list. Furthermore, the following rule should be observed: While one may use either a male or female character from one of the unusual lists, it is not a good idea to use both of them from the unusual lists. The reason for this is that a single unusual character may suggest almost the entire atmosphere for the story.

(3) The present formula will develop the popular love story. The love interest may be eliminated, if desired, by discarding operations 3 and 5. There are six supplementary formulas, specifically adapted for the writing of specialized types of stories, for use with the Genie, i. e.: (I) Romance Without Melodrama; (II) Action-Adventure Stories; (III) Detective-Mystery Stories; (IV) Comedy; (V) True Confession Stories; (VI) Short Short-Stories.

(4) One may write in his own LOCALE, CHARACTER, or both, and let the Genie supply the remainder of the plot—if requirements of a particular market are to be met.

(5) If one already has an idea—locale, character, situation—which he desires to use in the plot, it must of necessity be one or more of the nine elements contained in the Genie plot formula. Therefore, one may determine which one or ones are embraced by the idea—write it or them in the proper place or places on the Recording Sheet, and let the Genie supply the remainder of the structure. You may use this method for pepping up the plots of rejected stories.

(6) If the Genie formula promises to introduce too much plot, or too involved a plot, one should first complete the operation and plot structure, then discard what is not wanted. Do not apply the process of elimination until after the first 250 word plot synopsis is developed and written on the Recording Sheet. This is important!

(7) Just because a plot assignment given by the Genie looks impossible or difficult, do not discard it, but for your own satisfaction proceed to work it out until you have created a plot embracing the material at hand. Many of those which at first appear to have the least promise actually provide the most interesting and novel story plots. The Plot Genie will not furnish a structure that cannot be developed into a logical and perfect plot.

(8) Should the Genie suggest an element which violates a requirement of a particular market, or a situation which is undesirable in a certain story, another may be substituted.

(9) One should not attempt to build a plot until all the nine numbers which call for the elements are obtained. The structure should then be studied as a whole before the synopsis is written. Do not attempt to form a conclusion as to the practical merits of the Plot Genie until you have actually developed a dozen or more story plots with it.

The Operation of the Plot Genie

The operation of the Plot Genie is simple. The object is to have the mechanical device select a series of nine numbers which call for the requisite plot elements, one from each of the nine lists in the book.

Turn the disc three times and then observe what number shows through the slot, and then write this number in the proper space on the recording sheet. After having obtained the nine numbers—and not before—refer to the index book for your corresponding plot elements, and write these on the Recording Sheet opposite the proper number. The first number obtained by turning the disc three times supplies the locale; the second gives the principal male character, the third, the beloved, and so on.

Six Problems Lists

It will be observed that there are in the index six lists of "Problems," each containing 180. Therefore, on the fourth operation, or the selection of a problem, the following rule should be observed as a means of determining which of the six lists of "Problems" will be used: TURN THE DISC AGAIN UNTIL A NUMBER ENDING IN 1, 2, 3, 4, 5, or 6 APPEARS, AND LET THAT NUMBER INDICATE WHICH OF THE SIX PROBLEM LISTS TO USE. For instance, the number 152 would indicate that "List 2" is to be used; or, "List 5" would be used if the number 95 shows in the slot, and so on.

If, however, with this turn of the disc a number ending in 7, 8, 9, or 0 shows in the slot, turn the disc again until a number ending in 1, 2, 3, 4, 5, or 6 is obtained.

In the event that the disc stops between two numbers, the rule is that the disc should be turned a little further until the next number in sight occupies the slot.

Having obtained the necessary nine elements, the plot structure should be studied carefully as a whole, and then one should proceed to develop the first synopsis of the plot. Again, I want to urge you not to discard the outline before you, or not to be discouraged with it because it may look difficult or impossible. The very fact that some strenuous mental exercise is required on your part to justify the relationship between the nine elements at hand is a guarantee that having accomplished this you will have a plot structure that is novel and refreshing. It will be so because it will be different from the usual thing which has been done so many times.

You will observe in considering the fusing together of the nine plot elements which you have before you, that any one of them may suggest atmosphere or action that is so predominating it will practically determine the nature of the entire plot structure. Characters suggest situations and atmosphere, while locale and dramatic situations also suggest characters. The Genie plot formula, it will be observed, calls for the introduction of only two characters, a lover and a beloved. The locale and conflict which surrounds these two characters invariably suggests a "villain," or the necessary menace, in the form of a third principal character. Still other inconsequential characters will be suggested by the chain of dramatic situations which develop in the course of the construction of the plot. Thus it will be seen that by using the perfect system of starting with a single situation and two characters and by introducing all others as direct or indirect results of the presence of these, the Plot Genie can not do otherwise than build a perfect plot. There will be no unnecessary characters or extraneous situations, loose ends, or "blind alleys," and you may be assured that you will have a dramatic plot and not merely a rambling narrative such as results from the efforts of the average amateur writer.

In the perfect dramatic plot there should be no character nor dramatic situation introduced which does not in some manner bear a direct or indirect relationship to every other character and situation in the story.

Another important thing to be remembered by the operator, or writer, is that after the first plot structure is completed, it may be necessary in the second story synopsis to begin the story at some point far removed from the first situation suggested by the Plot Genie in the outline. The discovery may also be made that it is desirable to make some character other than the first suggested by the Plot Genie as the hero or the heroine. For instance, it may be a son, daughter, brother, sister, father, other relative, or even a friend, whose presence in the story will be suggested by the necessity of attaining certain specific results. In some instances it may even transpire that the first character suggested by the Plot Genie, or even the "beloved" may develop to be the menace when the story is completd. It all depends upon the turn of the imagination of the writer.

Example of How a Story Is Written
With the Plot Genie

Following the instructions under the "Operation of the Plot Genie," let us actually build a story.

We are first going to let the Plot Genie supply us with nine numbers by turning the disc three times for each one, as hereinbefore described— bearing in mind that we have to make an extra turn after Operation Number 4 in order to get the problem list together. Also, let us determine in advance that we are going to select our first two characters—our lover and beloved—from the "Usual" lists.

Following is the outline with which the Plot Genie supplies us:

Plot Requisite	Genie Number	Suggestions (From Index Book)
LOCALE	5	Farm
CHARACTER	153	Publisher
THE BELOVED	62	Mystic's daughter.
PROBLEM	44-4	Obliged to recover lost information or clue opposed by distance.
LOVE OBSTACLE	62	Beloved doubts the endurance of the lover.
COMPLICATION	136	An illicit love affair threatens loss of happiness to a loved one.
PREDICAMENT	9	Abduction is threatened by parties desiring valuable information.
CRISIS	77	Learn that a loved one is a murderer.
CLIMAX	29	Wherein the slain or wounded loved one proves to be the enemy in disguise.

Brief Synopsis

A magazine publisher has occasion to make a trip into the country and to stop at a farm house. His mission involves the discovery of important information which necessitates his covering a great distance in order to obtain this information. In the meantime he meets and falls in love with the daughter of an old mystic who is also interested in obtaining the same information which he seeks. There is a rift between them, and the situation develops wherein she doubts his endurance, and this is complicated when an illicit love affair threatens to seriously affect her happiness. She is threatened with abduction by enemies who are also concerned with the valuable information which is sought. A murder is committed and the crime is laid at the feet of the publisher. A terrific fight follows in which a man, at first thought to be the hero, is mortally wounded. It later develops, however, that the dying man is the enemy leader who has taken the place of the hero. A dying confession or other evidence points to him as the murderer, which absolves the hero. The valuable information which has been sought is discovered in the meantime, and the hero and heroine are united in happiness.

That is a promising little synopsis, but it is full of gaps. There are many questions to be answered, and it will be interesting figuring them out. The best part of it is that when we get through we will have a story plot that is perfect. The Genie has told us WHAT HAS HAPPENED, and now we ask, "HOW COULD IT HAPPEN THAT WAY?" Here is where our creative minds get some good exercise.

Questions to be Answered

1. What kind of lost information is it that is sought?
2. Why does the hero go to a farmhouse in search of it?
3. What is the nature of the farm?
4. Where is it located?
5. What does the fact that the first character is a publisher have to do with the story?
6. How does the publisher get acquainted with the girl?
7. What part does the mystic—the girl's father—play in the story?
8. Is he really the girl's father?
9. What kind of a mystic is he?
10. Does he use his mystic power?
11. Is he a real or a fake mystic?
12. Is he a friend or an enemy of the publisher?
13. How was the valuable information lost?
14. If by enemies, who were the enemies?
15. What was their motive?
16. Why did the matter of distance stand in the way of the publishers' restoring the lost information?
17. Is the distance over water, mountains, through swamps, forests, across

plains, in the bowels of the earth, or where?
18. How does the publisher set about to overcome the problem of distance?
19. How does the hero learn that the girl doubts his endurance?
20. Why does the girl doubt his endurance?
21. Is it his physical, mental, or moral endurance that she doubts?
22. Between whom is the illicit love affair which threatens the happiness of the girl?
23. In what way does it threaten her happiness?
24. How is the menace which is threatened by the illicit love affair removed?
25. Who removes it?
26. What does the enemy hope to gain by abducting the girl?
27. Is, or is not the girl abducted?
28. If not, who prevents it and how?
29. If so, who rescues her and how?
30. Who is murdered?
31. How is the murder committed?
32. Why was the publisher accused of having committed the murder?
33. What serious result is threatened on account of the publisher's being accused of the murder?
34. Why does the enemy take the place of the hero?
35. How is the enemy mortally wounded?
36. How is the hero cleared of the murder charge?
37. Does the hero or the girl approach the discovery of the lost information or clue at any time during the story?
38. If so, how many times?
39. How do they approach it?
40. How are they prevented from recovering the desired information or clue?

After the Idea is Digested

I have found from experience that after the Plot Genie supplies the skeleton framework for a story plot, it is a very good idea to let this digest for a day or two. In other words, "sleep on it" before going ahead and completing the story. In fact, that is exactly what I have done with this story and I think it would not be an exaggeration for me to say that there are at least a dozen different ways of developing this particular plot—all of them good. Any writer who has creative imagination could take this particular plot framework and write at least that many stories from it. Again, if it were handed to a hundred different writers, no doubt each of them would be able to develop as many different stories from it as have been suggested to me.

There is one important thing that the writer should not overlook. It is that the finished plot should not contain any loose ends. In other words, it should be what we call "tight." By this I mean that all of the main action and dramatic situations therein should involve the principal characters. As an illustration, in the story we have in hand it would not be a good plan to introduce extraneous or unnecessary characters in order to use the situation where an illicit love affair is injected. Neither should unnecessary characters be introduced to be involved in any of the other dramatic situations suggested by the Genie; so we will bear in mind that we are going to give all of our principal action to our main characters in this story.

Cast of Characters

Our cast of characters to begin with is about as follows: (1)) the publisher, (2) the girl, (3) the mystic, and (4) the enemy.

As the first character is an elderly publisher, it is logical that he would receive manuscripts of stories. One of these might be of the "True Story" variety which deals with moonshining. In the meantime, let us assume that the whole country is being flooded with a supply of illicit alcohol which is coming from a secret source and that the Government has offered a huge sum of money for information which will disclose the source. After reading the manuscript the publisher is impressed with the idea that it contains a clue which might be well to follow up. He casually tells a friend about this, and the friend, a wealthy young chap who is an aviation enthusiast as well as a sportsman, and who has been trying to inveigle the publisher into a hunting trip for some time, becomes interested. The young chap uses this reward as an argument to induce his friend to accompany him on a combined trip for hunting and seeking the treasure.

In the city there is a theatrical team in which the man is of the Svengali type, a hypnotist and magician, and the girl, young and beautiful. She is his daughter. One of their acts is mind reading done by the girl after she has been placed in a state of hypnosis by the mystic.

There are several ways in which the mystic and his daughter could learn of the valuable clue, but it must be done logically. To have them learn of it accidentally through some source totally different from the publisher's office would be considered coincidental. Right here I want to warn the novice that it is not good form to drag either characters or situations in "by the heels," or to indulge in coincidence in the construction of a plot.

In every publishing house, there are clerks or "readers." It is logical that one of these in this particular publishing house, a young woman, say, might be acquainted with the mystic's daughter, and might have copied part of the manuscript dealing with the clue. She tells her friend about it, and the girl in turn conveys the information to her father. The mystic, being sorely pressed with financial obligations, hits upon the idea of using the girl's clairvoyance to assist him in the discovery of the information which will lead to the reward. Therefore, he and the girl go to the country.

In the meantime the publisher and his friend start by airplane on their hunting trip, after having made reservations for accommodations at an inn in the country near a deserted farm, where the first clue to the location of the moonshine plant is supposed to be found. Now we have our principal characters on the ground.

At the inn, the girl and the aviator meet and fall in love. In the meantime, the girl is also courted by another young man whom we shall call the enemy. A number of interesting bits of action can be introduced here to build up this love affair, and to establish a rivalry between the publisher's friend, the aviator (who has now developed into the leading man), and the enemy, whose identity we shall disclose later. The aviator takes the girl for a spin in his plane while the couple are watched jealously by the enemy rival.

Right now we must stop and do a little thinking. The Genie tells us that the girl is abducted, or an attempt is made to abduct her; that there is an illicit love affair, and also that the enemy substitutes for the hero. We must find a motive which would result in the development of these dramatic situations. Suppose the enemy is in the liquor "racket" and has a gang which is operating a huge still in the nearby mountains. This places our farm in a mountainous country. He might own a plane which is used in transporting the illicit liquor and doing scout work in looking for officers of the law. The girl might be sent out by her father and accidentally arrive at a location near the still, and discover it, not knowing that the young enemy has anything to do with it. When he, the enemy, receives the report from his man that the concealed still has been discovered by the girl, he would naturally be greatly alarmed. One of the things he would think of would be to have the girl abducted to prevent her disclosing the information.

In the meantime, the young aviator and the publisher would logically set in motion some plan to carry out the mission which brought them to the country, and one idea that suggested itself to me is that they would decide to look up the person who submitted the story. It is planned that the young aviator shall do this. It develops that the party who wrote the story is a married woman and in order to gain her confidence, the aviator would have to cultivate her acquaintance, and might induce her to go with him for an airplane ride. This would suggest the illicit love affair to the mystic's daughter, who is now very much in love with the aviator.

Three other situations which have been given to us by the Genie must now be considered. One of these is the one in which the girl doubts the endurance of the hero; the second is the commission of a murder of which the hero is suspected; and the third is the development of a wounded lover who turns out to be the enemy in disguise. The last one is easy. We have already suggested that the enemy has an airplane. Naturally, he would keep it hidden, and might appropriate the hero's ship; this, the hero would discover, and would pursue him in the other plane. A battle in the air would follow in which the enemy is shot down, and, inasmuch as he was flying the hero's plane, it would appear that the hero had fallen. The fight is being watched by the girl and the publisher. The fight might follow an attempt to abduct the girl which is frustrated by the hero.

Now, as to the proposition of the girl's doubting the endurance of the hero, there could very easily develop an angle to the story in which the enemy is portrayed as a very swaggering bully, who forces his attentions on the girl, and when he is reprimanded in a gentlemanly way by the aviator, offers to fight. A waggish townsman suggests that the fight be made a sporting event; the idea is approved, and it is planned that the two men, both of whom are athletes, shall engage in a battle of some kind. Immediately, the heroine is secretly alarmed, as she believes that the aviator will be defeated, but knows that if she tries to dissuade him, he will fight anyway. Nevertheless, she tries, and it makes him more determined than ever to give the enemy a good whipping, which, of course, he does.

We have not yet decided who it is that is going to be murdered so that we can accuse the aviator of the crime. Confining ourselves to the already described rule of giving all principal action and dramatic situations to our main characters, we will not introduce an unnecessary and extraneous character to be murdered. Instead of this, we will have the old mystic killed by the enemy. It would be logical that the girl should tell her father about having discovered the moonshine plant, and that the old man should decide to make an investigation of his own. He is closely watched by the enemy, who follows him that night in the aviator's plane and shoots the old man from the air . We can establish the fact earlier in the story that the old mystic had taken a dislike to the aviator, and now when his daugher finds him dying, he relates how he has been shot by the aviator, thus throwing suspicion on him.

It is after this that the enemy attempts to abduct the girl, is frustrated by the aviator, and then the fight in the air takes place, in which the enemy is shot down in the aviator's plane, while the girl and the publisher look on. At this stage of the story the girl believes the aviator to be the murderer of her father, but the publisher, being a friend of the latter, would naturally defend him.

The climax, of course, takes place when it is discovered that the man who has been shot down is really the enemy, and when his identity is disclosed, he makes a dying confession that he has killed the old man.

I think the reader will agree with me that we have worked out a fairly good plot for either a novel or a motion picture play—one which is full of action and thrills. I do not mean to say that this story is exceptional, but I believe it does afford absolute proof that the Plot Genie will aid in the development of a plot which would never have suggested itself to the imagination of the writer.

The operator of the Genie should bear in mind that this plot framework which we have developed is only one out of many million that can be built with the aid of the Plot Genie. As a story, it is still incomplete. Even after a synopsis is written it should be gone over again and again, interesting bits of dialogue, description and action added, which will round it out so completely that it would be no trouble to convert it into either a finished short story or a scenario continuity.

Our next step will then be to give names to our characters, and to write the first story synopsis.

Further Development

We will not proceed with the further development of the plot with which the Plot Genie has supplied us. No doubt there are many interesting bits of action which did not occur to us at this time, but which would suggest themselves to either the novelist or continuity writer were this plot developed in complete detail for publication or as a motion picture scenario.

The novelist would probably develop a story to this point and then lay out the story in chapters. Then he would develop each chapter in more complete detail, so that when all of them were finished and added together they would provide a book-length story with all of the necessary dialogue and description written in the past tense.

The scenario or continuity writer would divide the story into sequences and then into scenes in which only action and dialogue would be described, but as in the case of the novelist, he would carry the process of development on to a much more perfect state than the following synopsis:

Detailed Synopsis

Cast:

Elwood Parker, an elderly publisher.

Keith Durant, a wealthy young sportsman.

Zenda, an old mystic.

Pamela Wynne, daughter of the mystic.

George Barry, a moonshine king.

Anna Meggs, farmer's wife.

Dulcy, the Redbone girl.

Elwood Parker, a New York magazine publisher, and his friend, Keith Durant, a wealthy young sportsman, are in the former's private office when a clerk brings in an armful of manuscripts. Durant has just been importuning Parker to forget business for a while and go on a hunting trip with him. Durant is an aviation enthusiast and has an airplane of his own, about which he is telling his friend.

Parker remarks to Durant that many of the stories which they receive contain the outpourings of the hearts of those who are writing, and that some of them might even be well followed by a detective as he advances the theory that they contain actual clues to crimes that have been committed. This intrigues the interest of Durant and, reaching into a pile of the manuscripts, he extracts one and jokingly remarks: "Well, let's see what's in this one. It has a title which sounds interesting." Parker hastily reads the "thumb-nail" synopsis which has been prepared for him by one of his readers.

"What did I tell you?" he exclaims. "This very first one points to the possibility of a huge illicit liquor plant which may actually be in operation somewhere."

"That reminds me," said Durant, "that Uncle Sam is offering a hundred thousand dollar reward to anyone who discloses the source of the alcohol that is being unloaded in Chicago. Here is our chance to kill two birds with one stone—let's take the hunting trip and try to get the reward."

The result of the conversation is that it is agreed between the two friends that they will leave very soon for the Blue Ridge Mountains of Kentucky on a trip combining both hunting and detective work. The destination selected is the address of Anna Meggs, the woman who submitted the manuscript.

In the meantime, one of the girl clerks in the publisher's office overhears the conversation and becomes very much interested. She, in turn, that evening tells her friend, Pamela Wynne, about the story and the conversation between her employer and the sportsman. Pamela is the daughter of a mystic and she and her father comprise a team which for several years has played the various large vaudeville theatres with a mind reading act, in which the girl has been the subject ever since she was twelve years of age. The girl's father, who goes by the name of Zenda, is in dire circumstances, as are a great many other performers who have been deprived of employment by the advent of talking pictures, and he becomes interested in the girl's story.

Pamela is very sympathetic toward her father and suggests that they use their combined powers to obtain the $100,000 reward. At first the old man is dubious.

"Why, we would first have to go there, then come in contact with the people who know about this before we could tune in on their thoughts," Zenda explained to Pamela.

Pamela, who has been hiding away savings to pay for a course which would enable her to help her father financially, tells the old man about it, and offers to use her money to pay their expenses on the trip. It is with great reluctance that old Zenda finally consents, and the two plan the trip.

Some time later all our principal characters are gathered at a country hotel in the Kentucky mountains, and, in addition to those heretofore introduced, there is a swaggering young chap by the name of George Barry, who is an excellent dancer, and who pays a great deal of attention to Pamela. In the meantime, although old Zenda has taken a decided dislike to Keith Durant, he and the girl have grown very fond of each other. In fact, their attachment has grown so strong that George Barry notices, and watches with resentment when Keith takes Pamela for a hop in his plane.

After Pamela and her father have become fairly well acquainted with the other guests, they add their talent as entertainers to that of the rustic stringed orchestra, and astound the natives by some demonstrations in mental telepathy. The plan of the old man is to tune in on the minds of these people in search of the clue he desires. The performance proves highly interesting for all the guests, and some very ridiculous situations result from it.

That very evening there is an open breach between Durant and Barry when the latter attempts to bully Pamela. When it looks as though there is going to be an immediate fight between the two, a wag in the crowd suggests that inasmuch as Pamela and her father have entertained the guests, the fight should be a sporting event for the further entertainment of the guests. Barry is sullen and insulting, while Durant shows his sportsmanship by agreeing to the proposal. He further stipulates that Barry should choose his own form of contest. Pamela is much alarmed and shows it when Barry retorts that it shall be a wrestling match, and that he will "break Durant in half." The event is planned for a few evenings later.

Durant's feelings are hurt when he learns that Pamela doubts his ability, and, as the time draws near for the contest, we see Barry slyly rubbing his body with the bark of a certain tree to induce excessive perspiration, so that Durant will be unable to hold him. He has been told of this trick by a Redbone girl.

We will pause here to explain that there is a race of people in certain parts of the South known as "Redbones," who are neither Indians nor Negroes, but who have the characteristics of both races. Usually, these people live in colonies, and it is one of these girls, whose name is Dulcy, who is in love with George Barry.

Dulcy's father and some other Redbones are employed by Barry to operate his battery of stills.

On the night of the wrestling match, there is a terrific struggle, in which Durant all but loses, but finally the match is declared a draw, and Barry hisses in Durant's ear that he will "get him some other way."

The next day, although she cannot explain why, Pamela is impelled to go for a stroll into the mountains alone, and is led right to the alcohol plant, but is frightened away. One of the Redbone men reports the matter to Barry, and he resolves to abduct the girl.

Keith Durant reminds the old publisher of the object of their mission, and it is decided that instead of the two calling together at the farm of Anna Meggs, that Keith shall go alone and apparently drop in by accident while out hunting. They fear that the woman will become suspicious.

When Pamela learns that Keith is making visits to the Meggs woman, who is known to be a divorcee with none too good a reputation, she misunderstands his intentions and doubts his fidelity, and this causes her to snub him, an attitude which he cannot understand.

In the meantime, Dulcy, the Redbone girl, also grows jealous of the attention that Barry is paying to Pamela, and when she reminds Barry that he has promised to marry her if she would keep his cabin for him, he pushes her away angrily and it can be seen that there is vengeance in her heart.

One evening when old Zenda starts out to make some investigations for himself with regard to the alcohol plant, he is watched by Barry, who suddenly conceives a fiendish plot to get rid of Keith Durant and the old man at the same time. Barry is an aviator himself, and has a number of planes which are used in transporting the alcohol. He knows that Durant is away temporarily, and so he steals Durant's plane and follows old Zenda. Watching his opportunity, he shoots the old man from the air. (The reader is left in doubt as to who shoots the old man, as the pilot of Durant's plane will naturally be suspected of having done the killing.)

Dulcy finds old Zenda, brings him in on a sled, although she is non-committal about how he has been wounded. The old mystic accuses Keith and describes how he was shot from above. Pamela is naturally grief stricken, and will permit Keith to neither help her nor minister to her father, who dies a few hours later.

In the meantime, Barry is determined to abduct Pamela and makes an attempt to do so, but is frustrated by Keith.

Barry learns that Durant knows about the alcohol plant and makes an attempt to get him with Keith's plane. Just as the plane leaves the ground with Durant in full pursuit, the latter swings aboard, and the two men are soon fighting a desperate battle in the air while others watch from the ground.

In the meantime, the publisher has extracted a confession from Dulcy that it was Barry who killed Zenda.

As the men fight furiously in the air for control of the plane, it dips, dives, sideslips, tailspins, and finally breaks into flames. While Keith is disengaging himself from the perilous position where he has fallen from one of Barry's blows, the latter seizes the parachute and jumps, leaving Keith to perish with the burning plane. Barry's chute fails to open, and he is killed. Keith takes the control of the plane, and with superhuman effort goes into a series of sideslips and brings the plane down, all but losing his life.

Of course, all misunderstandings are cleared between Pamela and Keith, and she not only wins the reward of $100,000, but a good husband as well.

The end

Conclusion

The foregoing synopsis is just such a one as I have sold to studios. It contains a sufficient amount of detailed description of plot and action to enable any competent continuity writer in the studio to develop a completed script.

By a study of it, the reader will be able to observe that not only has the process of unfolding or development continued throughout the writing of this revised synopsis, but it even introduces one of the principal characters. Reference is made here to the "Redbone" girl, Dulcy, whose presence in the story is required by the development of a situation. She not only provides an interesting character and one which strengthens the plot and adds more color to it, but her introduction makes possible the addition of considerable "production value." By this I mean the introduction of the colony of Redbones which will provide an opportunity for some very colorful, interesting and educational scenes.

We have also strengthened the climax of the story, and "pepped up" the action in the closing scenes where we have the hero and the villain engaged in a fight in mid-air in a burning plane, and the chances are that the chap who writes the continuity for the screen version, would add a punch by having the girl carried away by some of the villain's men, so that the hero would have to rescue her after he escapes from the burning plane. (And no doubt he will take equal liberties with other situations throughout the story, building them up with every revision.) Following this, it is safe to say that when the script is placed in the hands of the director and actual production begins on the picture, he will think of many other improvements in the way of bits of business, dialogue, or dramatic situations which suggest themselves as the characters in the story come to life in the form of the actors.

All of this is meant to impress upon the mind of the reader that no story is perfected with one writing. Like everything else, it must be developed gradually, step by step. In other words, we might say that beginning with the plot, which is the mere bud, the story unfolds like a rose until it presents a perfect picture from every angle.

Of course, there must be a plot structure to begin with, and the more novel and interesting that is, the better will be the finished story. The Genie has done its duty when it supplies the framework, and we have proven conclusively in the demonstration just made in the story we have written here, that a creative imagination can be set in operation aided by the Plot Genie with the result that a very interesting and worthwhile story can be written— one that would never have suggested itself in any other way.

In closing, I will say that I feel confident that any student-author who will master the art of dramatic plot building and then devote the necessary time and effort to the completion of the story, cannot but succeed. If the Plot Genie proves to be nothing more than an instrument of getting the student-author started in the right direction, and providing him with a concrete method to follow, I shall feel very happy indeed.

The Plot Genie is not by any means to be considered a toy. It is a scientific device which will faithfully help you build thousands of interesting story plots. However, in giving your creative mind valuable and stimulating exercise it will provide you with a great deal of entertainment.

The Genie will lead you into rich, unexplored fields of valuable story material. It will take your mind out of the rut—lift your imagination from the worn grooves—give your thoughts wings with which to fly out of circumscribed territory to which they have been confined by personal experience, and remove all boundaries and limitations to your ability to create new combinations of ideas for all kinds of stories for stage, screen, radio, books, or magazines.

Work seriously and faithfully with the Genie, and you will find it to be the best collaborator you ever had.

Backgrounds or Locale

1. In Asia
2. At the Zoo
3. In the Navy
4. In a bank
5. On a farm
6. At a mine
7. By a lake
8. On a ship
9. At a fort
10. In India
11. In court
12. On the beach
13. On a yacht
14. Near a river
15. In the slums
16. On a ranch
17. By a bayou
18. On the docks
19. At a depot
20. In Dixie
21. At the harbor
22. In a colony
23. In Egypt
24. Back stage
25. At school
26. At the morgue
27. On the desert
28. At the seashore
29. At the circus
30. On the Amazon
31. In a canyon
32. On an island
33. In prison
34. In the swamp
35. On the plains
36. In Africa
37. In an office
38. At the Casino
39. On the Bowery
40. In Arabia
41. In the forest
42. In a castle
43. In a foundry
44. In a theatre
45. At a mission
46. At an airport
47. In college
48. In a caravan
49. In an asylum
50. In a factory
51. In a jungle
52. In a mansion
53. At a banquet
54. In an arsenal
55. In a museum
56. In the trenches

BACKGROUNDS
(CONTINUED)

57. In a submarine
58. At a festival
59. In a hospital
60. In an Academy
61. In Hawaii
62. At a hacienda
63. On the frontier
64. In a vineyard
65. In a dope den
66. At a dam site
67. In the orchard
68. In a ballroom
69. At a saw mill
70. In the mountains
71. On a plantation
72. In Argentine
73. At an army post
74. At West Point Military School
75. In a dance hall
76. In a gymnasium
77. On a train
78. In the bad lands
79. On a river
80. At a sanitorium
81. In the canebrake
82. In a paper mill
83. In a small town
84. In the South Seas
85. In the Legislature
86. In the oil fields
87. In the Near East
88. At a Masque ball

89. At a race track
90. At a speakeasy
91. At an auto camp
92. At a lighthouse
93. In the pine woods
94. On a sheep ranch
95. In a steel mill
96. In the Far North
97. In a prison camp
98. In the Alps
99. At a road house
100. At a dude ranch
101. At a power house
102. At a camp meeting
104. At a bandit camp
103. At a movie studio
105. At a field hospital
106. Among grain fields
107. At a custom house
108. On a wagon train
109. At a logging camp
110. In a wealthy home
111. At a ranger's camp
112. In a laboratory
113. In the railroad yards
114. At a radio station
115. At a haunted house
116. At a reform school
117. At a tribal village
118. In an artist's studio
119. On a country estate
120. In a savage country
121. In a back settlement

BACKGROUNDS
(CONTINUED)

122. In a department store
123. In the Flowery Kingdom
124. In a machine shop
125. In a newspaper office
126. At a wireless station
127. In a tropical garden
128. In the smugglers' cave
129. In the explorer's camp
130. At police headquarters
131. At a construction camp
132. In a deserted village
133. On an Indian reservation
134. In the financial district
135. In a spiritualistic hall
136. In the Everglades
137. In San Francisco China-town
138. In the Paris Latin Quarter
139. At an English manor house
140. At a polo game
141. At a tennis tournament
142. At a regatta
143. On a cattle ranch in Australia
144. On the high seas
145. In the Klondyke
146. At a summer resort
147. In the underworld
148. In a ghost town in the Sierras
149. In a church yard
150. In New England
151. In the Scottish Highlands
152. On the Riviera
153. At a country club
154. In the Catacombs
155. In a refugee camp
156. At a collegiate football game
157. In a passenger airliner
158. In a ruined abbey
159. At a night club
160. In the Ghetto
161. On a houseboat
162. In Greenwich Village
163. In the Polar regions
164. On the golf links
165. In the North Woods
166. At a salmon cannery
167. At a hunting lodge
168. In the World War
169. On a rum-running boat
170. In the Bermudas
171. In an Irish fishing village
172. In a trapper's cabin
173. At a prize fight
174. At Secret Service Head-quarters
175. During the Mardi Gras
176. At a French chateau
177. In a penthouse
178. At a gambling hall
179. In a small town hotel
180. At a Fraternity House

Usual Male Characters

1. Spy
2. Diver
3. Guide
4. Judge
5. Gypsy
6. Miner
7. Nomad
8. Nurse
9. Pilot
10. Jockey
11. Racer
12. Clerk
13. Scout
14. Poet
15. Clown
16. Trapper
17. Bandit
18. Ranger
19. Banker
20. Consul
21. Artist
22. Bishop
23. Cowboy
24. Farmer
25. Actor
26. Beggar
27. Magician
28. Tailor
29. Gunner
30. Sailor
31. Dancer
32. Editor
33. Warden
34. Trader
35. Singer
36. Hunter
37. Broker
38. Cobbler
39. Soldier
40. Gymnast
41. Barber
42. Gambler
43. Peddler
44. Rancher
45. Waiter
46. Acrobat
47. Chemist
48. Burglar
49. Fireman
50. Cashier
51. Assayer
52. Doctor
53. Florist
54. Sheriff
55. Aviator
56. Convict

(CONTINUED)

57.	Invalid	89.	Manufacturer
58.	Printer	90.	Navy officer
59.	Athlete	91.	Automobile racer
60.	Servant	92.	Photographer
61.	Gangster	93.	Homesteader
62.	Surveyor	94.	Press agent
63.	Governor	95.	Timekeeper
64.	Merchant	96.	Caretaker
65.	Vagabond	97.	Telegrapher
66.	Bondsman	98.	Halfbreed
67.	Inventor	99.	Taxi driver
68.	Director	100.	Mining engineer
69.	Autocrat	101.	Radio singer
70.	Captain	102.	Electrician
71.	Composer	103.	Interpreter
72.	Explorer	104.	Moonshiner
73.	Bell boy	105.	Coast guard
74.	Smuggler	106.	Equestrian
75.	Merchant	107.	Missionary
76.	Humorist	108.	Adventurer
77.	Reporter	109.	Journalist
78.	Scholar	110.	Millwright
79.	Submarine officer	111.	Specialist
80.	Jazz orchestra leader	112.	Astrologer
81.	Lighthouse tender	113.	Evangelist
82.	Singing master	114.	Playwright
83.	Customs officer	115.	Statesman
84.	School teacher	116.	Realtor
85.	Administrator	117.	Capitalist
86.	Aeronautical engineer	118.	Fisherman
87.	Army officer	119.	Clergyman
88.	Backwoodsman	120.	Blacksmith

USUAL MALE CHARACTERS

121.	Cartoonist	151.	Prospector
122.	Prosecutor	152.	Machinist
123.	Novelist	153.	Publisher
124.	Auctioneer	154.	Architect
125.	Commandant	155.	Cattleman
126.	Aristocrat	156.	Bank teller
127.	Biographer	157.	Performer
128.	Contractor	158.	Detective
129.	Cameraman	159.	Chauffeur
130.	Technician	160.	Attorney
131.	Mine owner	161.	Druggist
132.	Instructor	162.	Costumer
133.	Astronomer	163.	Midshipman
134.	Accountant	164.	Nobleman
135.	Sportsman	165.	Foreman
136.	Lumberman	166.	Pugilist
137.	**Bohemian**	167.	Auditor
138.	Geologist	168.	Promoter
139.	Candidate	169.	Violinist
140.	Scientist	170.	Constable
141.	Forester	171.	Railroad engineer
142.	Librarian	172.	Auto mechanic
143.	Hypnotist	173.	Air mail pilot
144.	Lifeguard	174.	Radio announcer
145.	Policeman	175.	Draughtsman
146.	**Salesman**	176.	Golf champion
147.	Newsboy	177.	Carpenter
148.	Executive	178.	Civil engineer
149.	**Collegian**	179.	Football hero
150.	Pianist	180.	Politician

Unusual Male Characters

1. Exporter
2. Botanist
3. Anarchist
4. Paymaster
5. Squatter
6. Ski jumper
7. Comedian
8. Treasurer
9. Gondolier
10. Archduke
11. Factor
12. Senator
13. Croupier
14. Settler
15. Pioneer
16. Philatelist
17. Tutor
18. Diplomat
19. Caveman
20. Lobbyist
21. Pacifist
22. Reformer
23. Dietician
24. Inn keeper
25. Sculptor
26. Invader
27. Driller
28. Courier
29. Epicure
30. Analyst
31. Outrider
32. Warlord
33. Physicist
34. Healer
35. Oarsman
36. Prophet
37. Wizard
38. Triplet
39. Cossack
40. Chef
41. Cavalryman
42. Chaplain
43. Mystic
44. Mandarin
45. Shipwright
46. Engraver
47. Pirate
48. Trumpeter
49. Harpooner
50. Gigolo
51. Matador
52. Historian
53. Powderman
54. Octoroon
55. Immigrant
56. Dictator
57. Furrier
58. Ringmaster

UNUSUAL MALE CHARACTERS
(CONTINUED)

59. Hermit
60. Impresario
61. Translator
62. Monarch
63. Statistician
64. Philosopher
65. Vigilante
66. Troubadour
67. Philanthropist
68. Animal trainer
69. Orientalist
70. Archaeologist
71. Spiritualist
72. Trophy hunter
73. Buccaneer
74. Racketeer
75. Messenger
76. Bookmaker
77. Arab
78. Hijacker
79. Swimmer
80. Rurale
81. Fencer
82. Poacher
83. Voyageur
84. Censor
85. Eskimo
86. Lancer
87. Faker
88. Apache
89. Sheik
90. Bibliophile

91. Cheer leader
92. Grocer
93. Lineman
94. Conductor
95. Shepherd
96. Prince
97. Ambassador
98. Surgeon
99. Communist
100. Dentist
101. Peon
102. Juror
103. Yogi
104. Cadet
105. Friar
106. Peasant
107. Juggler
108. Colonist
109. Palmist
110. Legionnaire
111. Watchman
112. Man-about-town
113. Vaudeville artist
114. Research chemist
115. Airplane mechanician
116. Sports editor
117. Taxidermist
118. Toreador
119. Evolutionist
120. Polo player
121. Member of Parliament
122. Mounted police

UNUSUAL MALE CHARACTERS
(CONTINUED)

123. Landscape gardener
124. College president
125. Captain of Industry
126. News photographer
127. Motion picture producer
128. Football coach
129. Tennis champion
130. Courtier
131. Deacon
132. Dragoon
133. Minstrel
134. Wrangler
135. Landlord
136. Recorder
137. Canoeist
138. Motion picture director
139. Interior decorator
140. Dramatic critic
141. Drawbridge tender
142. Curio collector
143. Tight rope walker
144. Glass blower
145. Artilleryman
146. Horticulturist
147. Airport manager
148. Coffee taster
149. Iconoclast
150. Navigator
151. Quartermaster
152. Bootlegger
153. Symphony orchestra leader
154. Secret Service operative
155. Graphologist
156. Stage director
157. Pipe organist
158. Accoustician
159. Lapidarist
160. Infantryman
161. Globe trotter
162. Balloonist
163. Revolutionist
164. Archbishop
165. Metallurgist
166. Beach comber
167. Egyptologist
168. Harbor master
169. Toxicologist
170. Psychoanalyst
171. Magnate
172. Appraiser
173. Art dealer
174. Criminalogist
175. Radio operator
176. Meteorologist
177. Baseball pitcher
178. U. S. Marine officer
179. Jiu-jitsu expert
180. Metaphysician

Usual Female Characters

(Beloved)

1. Countess	22. Journalist
2. Modiste	23. Aristocrat
3. Musician	24. Playwright
4. Athlete	25. Manicurist
5. Waitress	26. Saleswoman
6. Manikin	27. Movie star
7. Invalid	28. Divorcee
8. Duchess	29. Governess
9. Peasant	30. Cashier
10. Housemaid	31. Widow
11. Secretary	32. Heiress
12. Noblewoman	33. Actress
13. Chorus girl	34. Artist
14. Chambermaid	35. Dancer
15. Sportswoman	36. Model
16. Evangelist	37. Nurse
17. Society belle	38. Co-ed
18. Adventuress	39. Milliner
19. School teacher	40. Poetess
20. Stenographer	
21. Telephone operator	

41. Consul's	daughter or sister
42. Apache's	"	"	"
43. Broker's	"	"	"
44. Rancher's	"	"	"
45. Collegian's	"	"	"
46. Actor's	"	"	"
47. Guide's	"	"	"
48. Miner's	"	"	"
49. Nomad's	"	"	"
50. Dope addict's	"	"	"
51. Backwoodsman's	"	"	"
52. Racer's	"	"	"

USUAL FEMALE CHARACTERS
(CONTINUED)

53.	Judge's	daughter or sister	
54.	Clown's	,, ,, ,,	
55.	Juror's	,, ,, ,,	
56.	Faker's	,, ,, ,,	
57.	Scout's	,, ,, ,,	
58.	Wizard's	,, ,, ,,	
59.	Trader's	,, ,, ,,	
60.	Warden's	,, ,, ,,	
61.	Hunter's	,, ,, ,,	
62.	Mystic's	,, ,, ,,	
63.	Farmer's	,, ,, ,,	
64.	Gunman's	,, ,, ,,	
65.	Singer's	,, ,, ,,	
66.	Tailor's	,, ,, ,,	
67.	Gunner's	,, ,, ,,	
68.	Sailor's	,, ,, ,,	
69.	Miller's	,, ,, ,,	
70.	Peon's	,, ,, ,,	
71.	Sage's	,, ,, ,,	
72.	Spy's	,, ,, ,,	
73.	Baker's	,, ,, ,,	
74.	Diver's	,, ,, ,,	
75.	Artist's	,, ,, ,,	
76.	Cowboy's	,, ,, ,,	
77.	Doctor's	,, ,, ,,	
78.	Editor's	,, ,, ,,	
79.	Bandit's	,, ,, ,,	
80.	Banker's	,, ,, ,,	
81.	Publisher's	,, ,, ,,	
82.	Missionary's	,, ,, ,,	
83.	Constable's	,, ,, ,,	
84.	Merchant's	,, ,, ,,	
85.	Promoter's	,, ,, ,,	
86.	Sheriff's	,, ,, ,,	

USUAL FEMALE CHARACTERS
(CONTINUED)

87.	Janitor's	daughter	or	sister
88.	Soldier's	,,	,,	,,
89.	Gangster's	,,	,,	,,
90.	Professor's	,,	,,	,,
91.	Florist's	,,	,,	,,
92.	Beggar's	,,	,,	,,
93.	Colonist's	,,	,,	,,
94.	Convict's	,,	,,	,,
95.	Gambler's	,,	,,	,,
96.	Fireman's	,,	,,	,,
97.	Peddler's	,,	,,	,,
98.	Realtor's	,,	,,	,,
99.	Captain's	,,	,,	,,
100.	Chemist's	,,	,,	,,
101.	Trapper's	,,	,,	,,
102.	Athlete's	,,	,,	,,
103.	Cobbler's	,,	,,	,,
104.	Magician's	,,	,,	,,
105.	Pugilist's	,,	,,	,,
106.	Scientist's	,,	,,	,,
107.	Vagabond's	,,	,,	,,
108.	Reformer's	,,	,,	,,
109.	Juggler's	,,	,,	,,
110.	Squatter's	,,	,,	,,
111.	Golf champion's	,,	,,	,,
112.	Landlord's	,,	,,	,,
113.	Novelist's	,,	,,	,,
114.	Explorer's	,,	,,	,,
115.	Fiddler's	,,	,,	,,
116.	Shepherd's	,,	,,	,,
117.	Junkman's	,,	,,	,,
118.	Oil king's	,,	,,	,,

119.	Director's	daughter or sister	
120.	Acrobat's	" " "
121.	Statesman's	" " "
122.	Homesteader's	" " "
123.	Driller's	" " "
124.	Mine owner's	" " "
125.	Aviator's	" " "
126.	Cattleman's	" " "
127.	Composer's	" " "
128.	Ferryman's	" " "
129.	District Attorney's	" " "
130.	Exporter's	" " "
131.	French poilu's	" " "
132.	Druggist's	" " "
133.	Assayer's	" " "
134.	Customs officer's	" " "
135.	Radio operator's	" " "
136.	Globetrotter's	" " "
137.	Harbor master's	" " "
138.	Mounted policeman's	" " "
139.	Lighthouse tender's	" " "
140.	College President's	" " "
141.	Taxidermist's	" " "
142.	Rum runner's	" " "
143.	Taxi driver's	" " "
144.	Photographer's	" " "
145.	Impresario's	" " "
146.	Ringmaster's	" " "
147.	Contractor's	" " "
148.	Architect's	" " "
149.	Psychoanalyst's	" " "
150.	Orchestra leader's	" " "
151.	Coast Guard's	" " "
152.	Equestrian's	" " "

USUAL FEMALE CHARACTERS
(CONTINUED)

153.	Criminal's	daughter	or	sister
154.	Navy officer's	"	"	"
155.	Telegrapher's	"	"	"
156.	Radio announcer's	"	"	"
157.	Manufacturer's	"	"	"
158.	Geologist's	"	"	"
159.	Clergyman's	"	"	"
160.	Air mail pilot's	"	"	"
161.	Interpreter's	"	"	"
162.	Moonshiner's	"	"	"
163.	Sportman's	"	"	"
164.	Evangelist's	"	"	"
165.	Night club hostess'	"	"	"
166.	Restauranteur's	"	"	"
167.	Police officer's	"	"	"
168.	Hijacker's	"	"	"
169.	Specialist's	"	"	"
170.	Executive's	"	"	"
171.	Prosecutor's	"	"	"
172.	Fisherman's	"	"	"
173.	Governor's	"	"	"
174.	Football hero's	"	"	"
175.	Prospector's	"	"	"
176.	Politician's	"	"	"
177.	Counterfeiter's	"	"	"
178.	Army officer's	"	"	"
179.	Mining engineer's	"	"	"
180.	Tennis champion's	"	"	"

Unusual Female Characters

(Beloved)

1. Diva	29. Censor
2. Waif	30. Choir leader
3. Spy	31. Servant
4. Siren	32. Cocotte
5. Twin	33. Zoologist
6. Ayah	34. Acrobat
7. Agent	35. Palmist
8. Nomad	36. Florist
9. Queen	37. Fencer
10. Guide	38. Canvasser
11. Diver	39. Taxi dancer
12. Beggar	40. Editor
13. Critic	41. Aviatrix
14. Creole	42. Gang moll
15. Regent	43. Debutante
16. Juror	44. Registrar
17. Duenna	45. Scenarist
18. Trader	46. Princess
19. Tomboy	47. Eurasian
20. Weaver	48. Costumer
21. Triplet	49. Lion tamer
22. Convict	50. Odalisque
23. Attorney	51. Seamstress
24. Houri	52. Hypnotist
25. Cowgirl	53. Senorita
26. Broker	54. Harpist
27. Geisha	55. Reporter
28. Mystic	56. Designer

UNUSUAL FEMALE CHARACTERS
(CONTINUED).

57. Gambler
58. Bookkeeper
59. Mind reader
60. Milk maid
61. Detective
62. Laundress
63. Nautch girl
64. Satirist
65. Recorder
66. Composer
67. Explorer
68. Bayadeer
69. Magdalen
70. Huntress
71. Reformer
72. Forewoman
73. Pacifist
74. Violinist
75. Hula girl
76. Bohemian
77. Botanist
78. Octoroon
79. Pianist
80. Dowager
81. Confectioner
82. Girl Scout
83. Immigrant
84. Tourist
85. Comedienne
86. Dietician
87. Radio singer
88. College Dean
89. Shop keeper
90. Clairvoyant
91. Bandit queen

92. Communist
93. Cave woman
94. Translator
95. Physician
96. Huckstress
97. Statistician
98. Anarchist
99. Gang leader
100. Innkeeper
101. Occultist
102. Novelist
103. Telegrapher
104. Appraiser
105. Astrologer
106. Biographer
107. Farmerette
108. Policewoman
109. Mountaineer
110. Press agent
111. Court reporter
112. Society editor
113. Chauffeuse
114. Linguist
115. Lecturer
116. Courtezan
117. Biologist
118. Charlatan
119. Political leader
120. Tennis champion
121. Interior decorator
122. Golf champion
123. Circus freak
124. Salvation Army lass
125. Beauty operator
126. Movie "Extra" girl

UNUSUAL FEMALE CHARACTERS

127. Cabaret entertainer
128. Booking agent
129. Factory worker
130. Orchestra leader
131. Motion picture director
132. Settlement worker
133. Social secretary
134. Blind girl
135. Club woman
136. Ranch owner
137. Manufacturer
138. Notary public
139. Antiques collector
140. Business executive
141. Music teacher
142. Pipe organist
143. Premiere danseuse
144. Suffragette
145. Radio entertainer
146. Psychoanalyst

147. Linotype operator
148. Factory worker
149. Trapeze performer
150. Historical character
151. Cotton picker
152. Ventriloquist
153. Hotel hostess
154. Elevator operator
155. Horticulturist
156. Equestrienne
157. Metaphysician
158. Tea room owner
159. Beauty prize winner
160. Snake charmer
161. Secret Service operative
162. Stage director
163. Night club hostess
164. Ship stewardess
165. Marathon dancer
166. Criminal decoy

167. Cossack's   daughter or sister
168. Mandarin's   ,,   ,,   ,,
169. Smuggler's   ,,   ,,   ,,
170. Hindoo adept's   ,,   ,,   ,,
171. Notorious woman's   ,,   ,,   ,,
172. Member of Parliament's   ,,   ,,   ,,
173. Chinese Tong leader's   ,,   ,,   ,,
174. Voyageur's   ,,   ,,   ,,
175. Factor's   ,,   ,,   ,,
176. Revolutionist's   ,,   ,,   ,,
177. Backwoodsman's   ,,   ,,   ,,
178. Archaeologist's   ,,   ,,   ,,
179. Vigilante's   ,,   ,,   ,,
180. Minstrel's   ,,   ,,   ,,

Problems

1. Desired fortune opposed by enemies.
2. Relief from stigma opposed by rivals.
3. Desired liberty opposed by suspicion.
4. A strike is threatened by poverty.
5. Desired health opposed by enemies.
6. Relief from habit opposed by friends.
7. A strike is threatened by insult.
8. Desired liberty opposed by rivals.
9. A mutiny is threatened by enemies.
10. A race war is threatened by rivals.
11. Relief from stigma opposed by friends.
12. Desired power opposed by rivals.
13. Relief from habit opposed by rivals.
14. A feud is threatened by enemies.
15. A boycott is threatened by rivals.
16. Desired fortune opposed by friends.
17. Relief from stigma opposed by enemies.
18. A feud is threatened by rivals.
19. A mutiny is threatened by poverty.
20. Desired liberty opposed by distance.
21. Relief from stigma opposed by poverty.
22. A revolution is threatened by rivals.
23. A mutiny is threatened by insult.
24. Desired power opposed by enemies.
25. A race war is threatened by insult.
26. Relief from pursuit opposed by rivals.
27. Desired fortune opposed by distance.
28. A boycott is threatened by insult.
29. Relief from stigma opposed by distance.
30. Desired health opposed by rivals.
31. Relief from pursuit opposed by friends.

32. A feud is threatened by poverty
33. Desired power opposed by suspicion.
34. A mutiny is threatened by rivals.
35. Relief from injury opposed by rivals.
36. A boycott is threatened by enemies.
37. Desired position opposed by rivals.
38. A race war is threatened by poverty.
39. Desired fortune opposed by suspicion.
40. Relief from sickness opposed by rivals.
41. A feud is threatened by oppression.
42. Desired liberty opposed by friends.
43. Relief from sickness opposed by enemies.
44. A feud is threatened by ignorance.
45. Desired fortune opposed by rivals.
46. Relief from habit opposed by poverty.
47. A boycott is threatened by poverty.
48. A race war is threatened by enemies.
49. Desired power opposed by friends.
50. Relief from stigma opposed by suspicion.
51. Desired liberty opposed by enemies.
52. Relief from sickness opposed by poverty.
53. A feud is threatened by superstition.
54. A revolution is threatened by poverty.
55. A boycott is threatened by ignorance.
56. A mutiny is threatened by superstition.
57. Desired position opposed by enemies.
58. Relief from sickness opposed by friends.
59. A mutiny is threatened by ignorance.
60. A revolution is threatened by insult.
61. Relief from suit opposed by poverty.
62. Desired power opposed by distance.
63. A revolution is threatened by enemies.
64. Desired position opposed by distance.

65. A boycott is threatened by superstition.
66. Desired position opposed by suspicion.
67. Relief from pursuit opposed by suspicion.
68. A mutiny is threatened by persecution.
69. A race war is threatened by ignorance.
70. Relief from oppression opposed by rivals.
71. Desired information opposed by friends.
72. Desired fame opposed by rivals.
73. A feud is threatened by insult.
74. Desired health opposed by friends.
75. A strike is threatened by enemies.
76. Desired fame opposed by distance.
77. A feud is threatened by persecution.
78. Desired health opposed by distance.
79. A mutiny is threatened by oppression.
80. Desired fame opposed by suspicion.
81. A strike is threatened by rivals.
82. Desired fame opposed by enemies.
83. A strike is threatened by oppresion.
84. Desired fame opposed by friends.
85. A strike is threatened by ignorance.
86. A rebellion is threatened by rivals.
87. A feud is threatened by fatal ambition.
88. A race war is threatened by oppression.
89. Desired health opposed by suspicion.
90. A strike is threatened by persecution.
91. Desired information opposed by rivals.
92. A family revolt is threatened by insult.
93. A strike is threatened by fatal ambition.
94. A family revolt is threatened by poverty.
95. Desired approbation opposed by rivals.
96. A rebellion is threatened by insult.
97. Desired fame opposed by danger to life.

98. A rebellion is threatened by poverty.
99. A family revolt is threatened by rivals.
100. Desired position opposed by friends.
101. Desired power opposed by danger to life.
102. Relief from prosecution opposed by rivals.
103. A rebellion is threatened by superstition.
104. Desired power opposed by legal procedure.
105. Relief from oppression opposed by enemies.
106. Desired liberty opposed by danger to life.
107. Relief by pursuit opposed by enemies.
108. A race war is threatened by fatal ambition.
109. Desired liberty opposed by legal procedure.
110. Relief from oppression opposed by friends.
111. A rebellion is threatened by ignorance.
112. Relief from pursuit opposed by distance.
113. Desired liberty opposed by duty to country.
114. A family revolt is threatened by enemies.
115. A strike is threatened by superstition.
116. Desired fame opposed by lack of money.
117. A rebellion is threatened by oppression.
118. Relief from sickness opposed by distance.
119. Desired fortune opposed by lack of money.
120. Relief from sickness opposed by suspicion.
121. Relief from habit opposed by distance.
122. A race war is threatened by persecution.
123. A boycott is threatened by oppression.
124. Desired information opposed by enemies.
125. Desired approbation opposed by suspicion.
126. Relief from injury opposed by friends.
127. A mutiny is threatened by fatal ambition.
128. A battle of sexes is threatened by insult.
129. A revolution is threatened by persecution.
130. Relief from oppression opposed by poverty.

131. Desired liberty opposed by lack of money.
132. A race war is threatened by superstition.
133. A battle of sexes is threatened by rivals.
134. A boycott is threatened by persecution.
135. Relief from oppression opposed by distance.
136. Desired power opposed by duty to country.
137. Relief from oppression opposed by suspicion.
138. Desired information opposed by distance.
139. Relief from imprisonment opposed by rivals.
140. Desired liberty opposed by duty to religion.
141. A rebellion is threatened by persecution.
142. A family revolt is threatened by ignorance.
143. Desired fortune opposed by danger to life.
144. Relief from habit opposed by suspicion.
145. A rebellion is threatened by loss of liberty.
146. Desired health opposed by danger to life.
147. Relief from imprisonment opposed by enemies.
148. A rebellion is threatened by enemies.
149. Desired power opposed by lack of money.
150. A strike is threatened by duty to country.
151. A rebellion is threatened by fatal ambition.
152. Relief from habit opposed by enemies.
153. A feud is threatened by duty to country.
154. Desired power opposed by false accusation.
155. Relief from injury opposed by suspicion.
156. A strike is threatened by loss of liberty.
157. A family revolt is threatened by superstition.
158. A rebellion is threatened by duty to country.
159. Desired fortune opposed by legal procedure.
160. Relief from imprisonment opposed by friends.
161. Desired liberty opposed by mental weakness.
162. A boycott is threatened by fatal ambition.
163. A mutiny is threatened by duty to country.

PROBLEMS
LIST ONE
(CONTINUED)

164. A feud is threatened by duty to loved ones.
165. A battle of sexes is threatened by poverty.
166. Desired power opposed by duty to religion.
167. Relief from injury opposed by poverty.
168. A mutiny is threatened by loss of liberty.
169. A race war is threatened by physical suffering.
170. Relief from imprisonment opposed by distance.
171. Desired position opposed by lack of money.
172. Desired fame opposed by duty to religion.
173. Relief from injury opposed by distance.
174. A revolution is threatened by oppression.
175. A religious uprising is threatened by insult.
176. Desired home or refuge opposed by friends.
177. Relief from persecution by rivals.
178. Desired accomplishment opposed by enemies.
179. Relief from persecution opposed by enemies.
180. Desired approbation opposed by distance.

PROBLEMS
LIST TWO

1. Relief from persecution opposed by poverty.
2. A boycott is threatened by duty to country.
3. Desired home or refuge opposed by suspicion.
4. A revolution is threatened by ignorance.
5. Desired accomplishment opposed by rivals.
6. A battle of sexes is threatened by enemies.
7. Desired approbation opposed by friends.
8. Relief from injury opposed by enemies.
9. Desired home or refuge opposed by enemies.
10. Relief from persecution opposed by distance.
11. A feud is threatened by duty to religion.
12. Desired home or refuge opposed by distance.

PROBLEMS
LIST TWO
(CONTINUED)

13. Relief from prosecution opposed by enemies.
14. Desired health is opposed by lack of money.
15. Relief from injury opposed by danger to life.
16. A feud is threatened by unjust accusation.
17. Relief from stigma opposed by danger to life.
18. A feud is threatened by physical suffering.
19. A revolution is threatened by superstition.
20. Desired accomplishment is opposed by distance.
21. A boycott is threatened by mental derangement.
22. Desired liberty is opposed by false accusation.
23. Relief from prosecution opposed by friends.
24. Desired power opposed by mental weakness.
25. Relief from prosecution opposed by poverty.
26. A mutiny is threatened by mental derangement.
27. Desired position opposed by danger to life.
28. Relief from persecution opposed by suspicion.
29. A mutiny is threatened by duty to religion.
30. Desired power opposed by physical weakness.
31. A boycott is threatened by loss of liberty.
32. A mutiny is threatened by unjust accusation.
33. Desired fortune opposed by duty to country.
34. Relief from pursuit opposed by danger to life.
35. A revolution is threatened by duty to country.
36. Desired fortune opposed by duty to religion.
37. Relief from stigma opposed by legal procedure.
38. Desired liberty opposed by lack of information.
39. Desired fortune opposed by inclement weather.
40. Relief from habit opposed by danger to life.
41. Desired fortune opposed by mental incapacity.
42. A boycott is threatened by duty to religion.
43. Desired power opposed by lack of influence.
44. A boycott is threatened by physical suffering.
45. Desired fortune opposed by false accusation.

PROBLEMS
LIST TWO
(CONTINUED)

46. A mutiny is threatened by duty to loved ones.
47. Desired fortune opposed by lack of information.
48. A battle of sexes is threatened by ignorance.
49. Desired liberty opposed by inclement weather.
50. Relief from sickness opposed by danger to life.
51. Desired fortune opposed by duty to loved ones.
52. Relief from imprisonment opposed by suspicion.
53. A race war is threatened by loss of liberty.
54. Desired power opposed by lack of facilities.
55. A race war is threatened by duty to country.
56. Desired power opposed by inclement weather.
57. A boycott is threatened by unjust accusation.
58. Desired position opposed by inclement weather.
59. Desired health opposed by legal procedure.
60. Relief from imprisonment opposed by poverty.
61. A feud is threatened by mental derangement.
62. Desired fortune opposed by lack of influence.
63. Relief from sickness opposed by legal procedure.
64. Desired liberty opposed by lack of influence.
65. Relief from stigma opposed by mental weakness.
66. Desired position opposed by mental weakness.
67. A mutiny is threatened by physical suffering.
68. Desired power opposed by lack of information.
69. Desired liberty opposed by lack of facilities.
70. Relief from persecution opposed by friends.
71. A boycott is threatened by duty to loved ones.
72. Desired fortune opposed by physical incapacity.
73. Relief from pursuit opposed by mental weakness.
74. A revolution is threatened by fatal ambition.
75. Desired liberty opposed by duty to loved ones.
76. Relief from pursuit opposed by legal procedure.
77. Desired fortune opposed by lack of facilities.
78. Relief from injury opposed by mental weakness.

PROBLEMS
LIST TWO
(CONTINUED)

79. A strike is threatened by duty to religion.
80. Desired power opposed by duty to loved ones.
81. Relief from injury opposed by duty to country.
82. A revolution is threatened by mental derangement.
83. Desired position opposed by physical weakness.
84. Relief from habit opposed by legal procedure.
85. A battle of sexes is threatened by persecution.
86. Relief from injury opposed by legal procedure.
87. Desired position opposed by lack of information.
88. Relief from injury opposed by false accusation.
89. A race war is threatened by duty to religion.
90. Desired position opposed by lack of influence.
91. Relief from stigma opposed by false accusation.
92. Desired position opposed by duty to country.
93. Desired health opposed by false accusation.
94. A boycott is threatened by unjust discrimination.
95. Desired information opposed by lack of money.
96. Desired fame opposed by lack of influence.
97. Desired health opposed by duty to country.
98. Desired information opposed by suspicion.
99. A strike is threatened by physical suffering.
100. Desired information opposed by danger to life.
101. Relief from prosecution opposed by suspicion.
102. Desired fame opposed by mental weakness.
103. Desired accomplishment opposed by friends.
104. Desired liberty opposed by physical weakness.
105. Relief from oppression opposed by legal procedure.
106. Desired accomplishment opposed by suspicion.
107. Desired fame opposed by physical weakness.
108. Desired health opposed by mental weakness.
109. Desired position opposed by duty to religion.
110. Relief from stigma opposed by duty to country.
111. Relief from habit opposed by duty to loved ones.

PROBLEMS
LIST TWO
(CONTINUED)

112. A revolution is threatened by physical suffering.
113. Relief from stigma opposed by inclement weather.
114. Desired fame opposed by duty to country.
115. Desired information opposed by lack of clue.
116. Desired health opposed by lack of information.
117. Desired position opposed by lack of facilities.
118. Relief from pursuit opposed by weakness.
119. Desired fame opposed by lack of information.
120. Desired health opposedby inclement weather.
121. A battle of sexes is threatened by oppression.
122. Desired position opposed by duty to loved ones.
123. Desired fame opposed by legal procedure.
124. A feud is threatened by loss of liberty.
125. Desired fame opposed by false accusation.
126. Desired position opposed by legal procedure.
127. Desired approbation opposed by danger to life.
128. Relief from sickness opposed by mental weakness.
129. Desired position opposed by false accusation.
130. A feud is threatened by unjust discrimination.
131. Desired home or refuge opposed by rivals.
132. Desired health opposed by physical weakness.
133. Desired fame opposed by lack of facilities.
134. A revolution is threatened by loss of liberty.
135. Desired fame opposed by duty to loved ones.
136. Relief from stigma opposed by lack of influence.
137. A feud is threatened by danger to life or health.
138. Desired information opposed by duty to country.
139. A rebellion is threatened by duty to religion.
140. Relief from pursuit opposed by false accusations.
141. Desired approbation opposed by lack of money.
142. A race war is threatened by duty to loved ones.
143. Desired fame opposed by inclement weather.
144. Desired information opposed by mental weakness.

PROBLEMS
LIST TWO
(CONTINUED)

145. Desired approbation opposed by enemies.
146. A revolution is threatened by duty to loved ones.
147. A strike is threatened by unjust accusation.
148. Desired health opposed by lack of influence.
149. Relief from sickness opposed by duty to religion.
150. Desired information opposed by legal procedure.
151. Desired health opposed by duty to loved ones.
152. Relief from sickness opposed by false accusation.
153. Desired approbation opposed by legal procedure.
154. Relief from stigma opposed by lack of facilities.
155. A revolution is threatened by physical suffering.
156. Relief from habit opposed by inclement weather.
157. A revolution is threatened by duty to religion.
158. Relief from habit opposed by false accusation.
159. Desired health opposed by lack of facilities.
160. Relief from sickness opposed by duty to loved ones.
161. A race war is threatened by mental derangement.
162. Relief from stigma opposed by duty to religion.
163. Desired health opposed by duty to religion.
164. Desired approbation opposed by false accusation.
165. A race war is threatened by unjust accusation.
166. Relief from sickness opposed by inclement weather.
167. Relief from injury opposed by duty to religion.
168. A battle of sexes is threatened by superstition.
169. Desired approbation opposed by duty to religion.
170. Relief from pursuit opposed by duty to religion.
171. Relief from prosecution opposed by distance.
172. A rebellion is threatened by unjust accusation.
173. Desired approbation opposed by mental weakness.
174. Relief from sickness opposed by lack of influence.
175. A strike is threatened by mental derangement.
176. Desired approbation opposed by duty to country.
177. Relief from oppression opposed by legal procedure.

PROBLEMS
LIST TWO
(CONTINUED)

178. Relief from pursuit opposed by duty to country.
179. A family revolt is threatened by persecution.
180. A religious uprising is threatened by poverty.

PROBLEMS
LIST THREE

1. A religious uprising is threatened by rivals.
2. A battle of sexes is threatened by danger to life or health.
3. Desired home or refuge opposed by lack of facilities.
4. Obliged to recover a lost person opposed by physicalweakness.
5. Desired vengeance against a cheater opposed by enemies.
6. Desired approbation opposed by lack of information.
7. Relief from oppression opposed by duty to religion.
8. Obliged to risk life in an effort to undertake a dangerous mission.
9. Desired vengeance against race, nation, or clan opposed by enemies.
10. Obliged to recover a lost person opposed by lack of influence.
11. Desired information opposed by physical weakness.
12. Relief from oppression opposed by danger to life.
13. A mutiny is threatened by unjust discrimination.
14. Obliged to risk liberty in an effort to apprehend a criminal.
15. Desired accomplishment opposed by false accusation.
16. A battle of sexes is threatened by unjust discrimination.
17. Obliged to risk life in an effort to engage in battle.
18. Relief from stigma opposed by lack of information.
19. A mutiny is threatened by danger to life or health.
20. A battle of sexes is threatened by loss of liberty.
21. Obliged to risk life in an effort to apprehend a criminal.
22. Desired home or refuge opposed by lack of information.
23. Relief from unjust accusation opposed by duty to loved ones.

24. Obliged to risk honor in an effort to brave a storm or cataclysm.
25. Desired information opposed by inclement weather.
26. Relief from pursuit opposed by lack of information.
27. A family revolt is threatened by fatal ambition.
28. Obliged to risk friendship in an effort to prove one's strength.
29. Desired vengeance against race, nation or clan opposed by rivals.
30. Relief from unjust accusation opposed by lack of facilities.
31. Desired approbation opposed by physical weakness.
32. Relief from sickness opposed by duty to country.
33. Obliged to prevent a terrible injustice opposed by danger to life.
34. A family revolt is threatened by duty to country.
35. A boycott is threatened by danger to life or health.
36. Obliged to risk health in an effort to brave deep waters.
37. Desired vengeance against opposite sex opposed by enemies.
38. Desired accomplishment opposed by lack of facilities.
39. Obliged to recover a lost person opposed by enemies.
40. Relief from pursuit opposed by lack of facilities.
41. Desired accomplishment opposed by danger to life.
42. Obliged to recover a lost person opposed by distance.
43. Desired information opposed by lack of influence.
44. Relief from pursuit opposed by duty to loved ones.
45. A race war is threatened by danger to life or health.
46. Obliged to risk health in an effort to brave an air voyage.
47. Desired vengeance against a rival in love opposed by rivals.
48. Desired home or refuge opposed by inclement weather.
49. Relief from oppression opposed by false accusation.
50. A race war is threatened by unjust discrimination.
51. Obliged to recover a lost person opposed by rivals.
52. Desired home or refuge opposed by physical weakness.
53. Relief from imprisonment opposed by lack of information.

PROBLEMS
LIST THREE
(CONTINUED)

54. A rebellion is threatened by danger to life or health.
55. Desired vengeance against a rival in love opposed by enemies.
56. Obliged to recover a lost person opposed by friends.
57. A battle of sexes is threatened by duty to loved ones.
58. Relief from imprisonment is opposed by lack of facilities.
59. Obliged to risk health in an effort to overthrow a monarch.
60. Relief from pursuit opposed by inclement weather.
61. Desired information opposed by duty to loved ones.
62. Relief from habit opposed by mental weakness.
63. Obliged to risk honor in an effort to put down a rebellion.
64. Desired approbation opposed by duty to loved ones.
65. Relief from stigma opposed by physical weakness.
66. Obliged to recover a lost person opposed by poverty.
67. Relief from sickness opposed by lack of information.
68. A religious uprising is threatened by loss of liberty.
69. Desired information opposed by duty to religion.
70. Relief from sickness opposed by physical weakness.
71. Obliged to recover a lost person opposed by lack of information.
72. Desired vengeance against race, nation, or clan opposed by poverty.
73. A battle of sexes is threatened by mental derangement.
74. Relief from prosecution opposed by danger to life.
75. Desired accomplishment opposed by duty to religion.
76. Obliged to solve a mysterious crime opposed by enemies.
77. A family revolt is threatened by unjust discrimination.
78. Desired information opposed by false accusation.
79. Relief from sickness opposed by lack of facilities.
80. A strike is threatened by unjust discrimination.
81. A battle of sexes is threatened by fatal ambition.
82. Obliged to risk honor in an effort to overthrow a monarch.
83. Relief from oppression opposed by lack of information.
84. Desired information opposed by lack of facilities.

PROBLEMS
LIST THREE
(CONTINUED)

85. Relief from imprisonment opposed by duty to country.
86. A strike is threatened by duty to loved ones.
87. Obliged to risk honor in an effort to engage in battle.
88. A battle of sexes is threatened by unjust accusation.
89. Obliged to solve a mysterious crime opposed by rivals.
90. Relief from prosecution opposed by legal procedure.
91. Desired approbation opposed by lack of faciilties.
92. Relief from imprisonment opposed by duty to loved ones.
93. Obliged to recover a lost person opposed by mental weakness.
94. Desired vengeance against race, nation or clan opposed by friends.
95. A religious uprising is threatened by unjust discrimination.
96. Relief from unjust accusation opposed by lack of information.
97. Desired approbation opposed by lack of influence.
98. A rebellion is threatened by physical suffering.
99. Relief from oppression opposed by physical weakness.
100. Desired home or refuge opposed by duty to country.
101. Obliged to solve a mysterious crime opposed by friends.
102. A rebellion is threatened by unjust discrimination.
103. Desired accomplishment opposed by legal procedure.
104. Relief from imprisonment opposed by inclement weather.
105. Obliged to recover lost valuables opposed by distance.
106. A religious uprising is threatened by duty to country.
107. Obliged to risk love in an effort to overthrow a monarch.
108. Desired home or refuge opposed by mental weakness.
109. Relief from oppression opposed by inclement weather.
110. Obliged to recover a lost person opposed by suspicion.
111. A strike is threatened by danger to life or health.
112. Obliged to risk honor in an effort to expose a vicious ring.
113. Relief from unjust accusation opposed by false accusation.
114. Desired home or refuge opposed by duty to loved ones.
115. Obliged to recover lost valuables opposed by inclement

weather.
116. A religious uprising is threatened by duty to loved ones.
117. Obliged to risk honor in an effort to brave an air voyage.
118. Desired accomplishment opposed by physical weakness.
119. Relief from imprisonment opposed by duty to religion.
120. Obliged to recover a lost person opposed by duty to country.
121. A religious uprising is threatened by danger to life or health.
122. Obliged to risk life in an effort to capture a vicious animal.
123. Desired vengeance against race, nation or clan opposed by distance.
124. Obliged to recover a lost person opposed by inclement weather.
125. Desired home or refuge opposed by lack of money.
126. A battle of sexes is threatened by duty to country.
127. Obliged to risk life in an effort to rescue an unfortunate.
128. Desired vengeance against the opposite sex opposed by danger to life.
129. Obliged to solve a mysterious crime opposed by duty to religion.
130. Desired vengeance against race, nation or clan opposed by physical weakness.
131. Obliged to restore health or happiness to a loved one opposed by distance.
132. Desired vengeance against a cheater opposed by danger to life.
133. Relief from unjust accusation opposed by inclement weather.
134. Desired home or refuge opposed by duty to religion.
135. Relief from imprisonment opposed by danger to life.
136. Desired accomplishment opposed by duty to country.
137. Obliged to recover lost valuables opposed by rivals.
138. A family revolt is threatened by duty to religion.
139. Desired approbation opposed by inclement weather.
140. Relief from imprisonment opposed by legal procedure.
141. Desired home or refuge opposed by false accusation.
142. A family revolt is threatened by duty to loved ones.

143. Relief from pursuit opposed by lack of influence.
144. Desired home or refuge opposed by danger to life.
145. Relief from oppression opposed by duty to country.
146. Obliged to recover lost valuables opposed by friends.
147. A revolution is threatened by unjust accusation.
148. A family revolt is threatened by oppression.
149. A religious uprising is threatened by enemies.
150. A rebellion is threatened by mental derangement.
151. Relief from stigma opposed by duty to loved ones.
152. Desired accomplishment opposed by lack of money.
153. Relief from oppression opposed by mental weakness.
154. Relief from habit opposed by duty to religion.
155. A religious uprising is threatened by oppression.
156. A rebellion is threatened by duty to loved ones.
157. Relief from habit opposed by duty to country.
158. A family revolt is threatened by loss of liberty.
159. Relief from unjust accusation opposed by distance.
160. Relief from injury opposed by physical weakness.
161. A battle of sexes is threatened by physical suffering.
162. Obliged to recover lost valuables opposed by duty to country.
163. Desired vengeance against a law breaker opposed by enemies.
164. Relief from prosecution opposed by lack of information.
165. Desired accomplishment opposed by duty to loved ones.
166. A revolution is threatened by danger to life or health.
167. Obliged to identify an unknown person opposed by suspicion.
168. Desired vengeance against a law breaker opposed by friends.
169. Relief from prosecution opposed by physical weakness.
170. Desired accomplishment opposed by lack of influence.
171. Obliged to recover lost valuables opposed by danger to life.
172. Obliged to risk liberty in an effort to rescue an unfortunate.
173. Relief from unjust accusation opposed by physical weakness.
174. Desired accomplishment opposed by inclement weather.
175. Relief from oppression opposed by lack of facilities.

PROBLEMS
LIST THREE
(CONTINUED)

176. Obliged to recover lost valuables opposed by mental weakness.
177. Desired vengeance against a law breaker opposed by false accusation.
178. Obliged to risk position in an effort to brave an air voyage.
179. A revolution is threatened by unjust discrimination.
180. A battle of sexes is threatened by duty to religion.

PROBLEMS
LIST FOUR

1. A religious uprising is threatened by persecution.
2. Obliged to risk life in an effort to overthrow a monarch.
3. A family revolt is threatened by danger to life or health.
4. Desired vengeance against the opposite sex opposed by friends.
5. Desired home or refuge opposed by lack of influence.
6. Relief from imprisonment opposed by false accusation.
7. Obliged to recover a lost person opposed by danger to life.
8. Relief from prosecution opposed by inclement weather.
9. Desired home or refuge opposed by legal procedure.
10. Relief from imprisonment opposed by lack of influence.
11. Obilged to recover lost information or clue opposed by friends.
12. A religious uprising is threatened by mental derangement.
13. Obliged to risk life in an effort to prove one's strength.
14. A religious uprising is threatened by unjust accusation.
15. Obliged to risk honor in an effort to rescue a loved one.
16. A family revolt is threatened by mental derangement.
17. Obliged to identify an unknown person opposed by friends.
18. Obliged to risk health in an effort to put down a rebellion.
19. Obliged to recover lost information or clue opposed by poverty.
20. Desired vengeance against an insulter opposed by suspicion.

21. A religious uprising is threatened by duty to religion.
22. Obliged to risk health in an effort to destroy a government.
23. Obliged to risk fortune in an effort to brave deep waters.
24. A religious uprising is threatened by fatal ambition.
25. Obliged to recover lost valuables opposed by lack of facilities.
26. Desired vengeance against an insulter opposed by inclement weather.
27. Obliged to risk health in an effort to brave a terrible disease.
28. Obliged to identify an unknown person opposed by false accusation.
29. Desired vengeance against a law breaker opposed by lack of influence.
30. Obliged to risk friendship in an effort to put down a rebellion.
31. Obliged to prevent a terrible injustice opposed by mental weakness.
32. Obliged to risk health in an effort to brave a storm or cataclysm.
33. Desired vengeance against the opposite sex opposed by legal procedure.
34. Obliged to prevent a terrible injustice opposed by false accusation.
35. Obliged to risk honor in an effort to apprehend a dangerous criminal.
36. Obliged to risk health in an effort to rescue an unfortunate.
37. Desired vengeance against opposite sex opposed by distance.
38. Obliged to prevent a terrible injustice opposed by suspicion.
39. Obliged to identify an unknown person opposed by danger to life.
40. Obliged to recover lost information or clue opposed by mental weakness.
41. Desired vengeance against a law breaker opposed by inclement weather.
42. Obliged to prevent a terrible injustice opposed by duty to

country.
43. Obliged to identify an unknown person opposed by lack of facilities.
44. Obliged to recover lost information or clue opposed by distance.
45. Relief from unjust accusation opposed by duty to religion.
46. Desired accomplishment opposed by lack of influence.
47. Relief from imprisonment opposed by physical weakness.
48. Obliged to recover lost valuables opposed by poverty.
49. Desired accomplishment opposed by mental weakness.
50. Obliged to recover lost information or clue opposed by rivals.
51. Obliged to risk health in an effort to prove one's strength.
52. A religious uprising is threatened by physical suffering.
53. Obliged to prevent a terrible injustice opposed by distance.
54. Obliged to risk happiness in an effort to prove one's strength.
55. Obliged to prevent a crime or injury opposed by danger to life.
56. Desired vengeance against a cheater opposed by false accusation.
57. Obliged to recover a lost person opposed by duty to loved ones.
58. Obliged to solve a mysterious crime opposed by mental weakness.
59. Obliged to prevent a crime or injury opposed by legal procedure.
60. Obliged to risk happiness in an effort to capture a vicious animal.
61. Desired vengeance against a cheater opposed by legal procedure.
62. Desired vengeance against a tyrant or oppressor opposed by lack of information.
63. Obliged to risk friendship in an effort to brave a maniac or insane person.
64. Obliged to prevent a terrible injustice opposed by lack of

- - - -

facilities.

65. Desired vengeance against a law breaker opposed by duty to religion.
66. Obliged to recover lost information or clue opposed by danger to life.
67. Desired vengeance against a cheater opposed by lack of facilities.
68. Obliged to prevent a crime or injury opposed by duty to country.
69. Obliged to risk liberty in an effort to expose a vicious ring.
70. Obliged to solve a mystery or phenomenon opposed by legal procedure.
71. Desired vengeance against a law breaker opposed by lack of information.
72. Obliged to risk happiness in an effort to undertake a dangerous mission.
73. Obliged to restore health or happiness to a loved one opposed by poverty.
74. Desired vengeance against one who has damaged a good name opposed by duty to religion.
75. Obliged to solve a mystery or phenomenon opposed by lack of facilities.
76. Desired vengeance against a cheater opposed by duty to religion.
77. Relief from persecution opposed by duty to loved ones.
78. Obliged to prevent a catastrophe opposed by distance.
79. Desired vengeance against the opposite sex opposed by rivals.
80. Obliged to recover a lost person opposed by lack of facilities.
81. Obliged to risk health in an effort to escape from punishment.
82. Desired vengeance against race, nation or clan opposed by danger to life.
83. Obliged to solve a mystery or phenomenon opposed by inclement weather.

PROBLEMS
LIST FOUR
(CONTINUED)

84. Desired vengeance against a cheater opposed by duty to loved ones.
85. Obliged to recover lost valuables opposed by lack of influence.
86. Relief from persecution opposed by lack of information.
87. A religious uprising is threatened by superstition.
88. Desired vengeance against one who has caused loss of valuables opposed by duty to country.
89. Relief from unjust accusation opposed by rivals.
90. Desired vengeance against one who has caused loss of valuables opposed by lack of facilities.
91. Obliged to restore health of happiness to a loved one opposed by duty to religion.
92. Desired vengeance against race, nation or clan opposed by lack of information.
93. Obliged to risk happiness in an effort to brave a maniac or insane person.
94. Obliged to prevent a terrible injustice opposed by duty to religion.
95. Desired vengeance against a rival in love opposed by friends.
96. Obliged to risk position in an effort to brave deep waters.
97. Obliged to recover lost valuables opposed by suspicion.
98. Relief from injury opposed by physical weakness.
99. Obliged to risk name in an effort to engage in battle.
100. A family revolt is threatened by unjust accusation.
101. Obliged to risk life in an effort to put down a rebellion.
102. Obliged to prevent a terrible injustice opposed by legal procedure.
103. Desired vengeance against one who has caused injury opposed by poverty.
104. Obliged to risk friendship in an effort to brave mental destruction.
105. Desired vengeance against a tyrant or oppressor opposed by duty to loved ones.

106. Obliged to restore health or happiness to a loved one opposed by legal procedure.
107. Desired vengeance against one who has damaged good name opposed by legal procedure.
108. Obliged to restore health or happiness to a loved one opposed by lack of facilities.
109. Desired vengeance against one who has caused loss of valuables opposed by lack of influence.
110. Relief from unjust accusation opposed by friends.
111. Desired vengeance against one who has caused loss of valuables opposed by duty to loved ones.
112. Obliged to restore health or happiness to a loved one opposed by duty to loved ones.
113. Desired vengeance against a tyrant or oppressor opposed by physical weakness.
114. Obliged to prevent a terrible injustice opposed by inclement weather.
115. Desired vengeance against a rival in love opposed by poverty.
116. Obliged to recover lost valuables opposed by false accusation.
117. Obliged to risk a fortune in an effort to engage in battle.
118. Obliged to risk name in an effort to apprehend a criminal.
119. Desired vengeance against a tyrant or oppressor opposed by friends.
120. Obliged to risk position in an effort to brave a storm or cataclysm.
121. Obliged to recover lost information or clue opposed by lack of information.
122. Desired vengeance against a law breaker opposed by physical weakness.
123. Obliged to risk love in an effort to expose a vicious ring.
124. Desired vengeance against a rival in love opposed by distance.
125. Obliged to restore health or happiness to a loved one opposed by friends.
126. Desired vengeance against one who has damaged good name

opposed by rivals.

127. Obliged to risk friendship in an effort to undertake a dangerous mission.
128. Desired vengeance against a tyrant or oppressor opposed by rivals.
129. Obliged to risk fortune in an effort to rescue a loved one.
130. Relief from persecution opposed by lack of facilities.
131. Obliged to risk honor in an effort to prove one's strength.
132. Obliged to prevent a catastrophe opposed by danger to life.
133. Desired vengeance against the opposite sex opposed by mental weakness.
134. Obliged to risk health in an effort to brave a maniac or insane person.
135. Desired vengeance against race, nation or clan opposed by suspicion.
136. Obliged to risk position in an effort to escape from imprisonment.
137. Desired vengeance against the opposite sex opposed by suspicion.
138. Obliged to risk fortune in an effort to rescue an unfortunate.
139. Relief from persecution opposed by inclement weather.
140. A religious uprising is threatened by ignorance.
141. Desired vengeance against one who has damaged good name opposed by lack of influence.
142. Obliged to restore health or happiness to a loved one opposed by suspicion.
143. Obliged to risk fortune in an effort to brave an air voyage.
144. Obliged to prevent crime or injury opposed by rivals.
145. Desired vengeance against one who has caused loss of valuables opposed by physical weakness.
146. A family revolt is threatened by physical suffering.
147. Obliged to prevent a terrible injustice opposed by enemies.
148. Obliged to identify an unknown person opposed by duty to country.

149. Desired vengeance against one who has damaged good name opposed by distance.
150. Obliged to risk friendship in an effort to brave an air voyage.
151. Desired vengeance against race, nation or clan opposed by mental weakness.
152. Obliged to risk name in an effort to undertake a dangerous mission.
153. Desired vengeance against a tyrant or oppressor opposed by duty to country.
154. Obliged to restore health or happiness to a loved one opposed by false accusation.
155. Desired vengeance against one who has caused loss of valuables opposed by mental weakness.
156. Relief from injury opposed by inclement weather.
157. Desired vengeance against one who has damaged good name opposed by lack of facilities.
158. Obliged to restore health or happiness to a loved one opposed by danger to life.
159. Desired vengeance against a law breaker opposed by lack of facilities.
160. Obliged to solve mysterious crime opposed by physical weakness.
161. Relief from injury opposed by lack of information.
162. Obliged to recover lost valuables opposed by legal procedure.
163. Obliged to prevent a terrible injustice opposed by poverty.
164. Obliged to risk name in an effort to overthrow a monarch.
165. Relief from unjust accusation opposed by danger to life.
166. Obliged to identify an unknown person opposed by enemies.
167. Desired vengeance against the opposite sex opposed by poverty.
168. Obliged to recover lost information or clue opposed by duty to country.
169. Desired vengeance against one who has caused injury opposed by physical weakness.
170. Obliged to risk health in an effort to undertake a dangerous

PROBLEMS
LIST FOUR
(CONTINUED)

mission.

171. Desired vengeance against one who has caused injury opposed by legal procedure.
172. Desired vengeance against one who has caused loss of valuables opposed by false accusation.
173. Desired vengeance against one who has caused loss of valuables opposed by duty to religion.
174. Desired vengeance against race, nation or clan opposed by legal procedure.
175. Obliged to risk love in an effort to rescue a loved one.
176. Relief from prosecution opposed by duty to loved ones.
177. Obliged to risk liberty in an effort to overthrow a monarch.
178. Desired vengeance against the opposite sex opposed by lack of information.
179. Obliged to risk happiness in an effort to escape from imprisonment.
180. Desired vengeance against one who has caused injury opposed by duty to loved ones.

PROBLEMS
LIST FIVE

1. Desired vengeance against race, nation or clan opposed by inclement weather.
2. Obliged to risk honor in an effort to brave a maniac or insane person.
3. Vengeance against a tyrant or oppressor opposed by suspicion.
4. Obliged to risk liberty in an effort to undertake a dangerous mission.
5. Desired vengeance against a rival in love opposed by duty to country.
6. Obliged to risk position in an effort to brave mental destruction.
7. Desired vengeance against one who has damaged good name opposed by friends.

8. Obliged to risk fortune in an effort to escape from imprisonment.
9. Desired vengeance against a cheater opposed by lack of influence.
10. Obliged to risk position in an effort to brave a terrible disease.
11. Desired vengeance against the opposite sex opposed by duty to country.
12. Obliged to prevent a terrible injustice opposed by physical weakness.
13. Desired vengeance against a rival in love opposed by inclement weather.
14. Obliged to solve a mysterious crime opposed by distance.
15. Desired vengeance against the opposite sex opposed by false accusation.
16. Obliged to prevent a catastrophe opposed by lack of facilities.
17. Desired vengeance against race, nation or clan opposed by lack of influence.
18. Obliged to risk friendship in an effort to escape from imprisonment.
19. Desired vengeance against a cheater opposed by poverty.
20. Obliged to recover a lost person opposed by duty to religion.
21. Desired vengeance against a rival in love opposed by danger to life.
22. Obliged to risk friendship in an effort to brave deep waters.
23. Desired vengeance against a law breaker opposed by mental weakness.
24. Obliged to risk health in an effort to expose a vicious ring.
25. Desired vengeance against race, nation or clan opposed by duty to religion.
26. Obliged to restore health or happiness to a loved one opposed by rivals.
27. Desired vengeance against a tyrant or oppressor opposed by enemies.
28. Obliged to risk liberty in an effort to brave a maniac or insane

person.
29. Desired vengeance against the opposite sex opposed by inclement weather.
30. Obliged to risk love in an effort to brave a storm or cataclysm.
31. Desired vengeance against a rival in love opposed by false accusation.
32. Obliged to risk friendship in an effort to capture a vicious animal.
33. Desired vengeance against race, nation or clan opposed by false accusation.
34. Obliged to risk happiness in an effort to brave mental destruction.
35. Desired vengeance against a tyrant or oppressor opposed by poverty.
36. Obliged to risk position in an effort to overthrow a monarch.
37. Desired vengeance against a rival in love opposed by legal procedure.
38. Obliged to risk health in an effort to brave mental destruction.
39. Desired vengeance against opposite sex opposed by duty to loved ones.
40. Obliged to restore health or happiness to a loved one opposed by mental weakness.
41. Desired vengeance against one who has caused loss of valuables opposed by rivals.
42. Obliged to risk position in an effort to brave a maniac or insane person.
43. Desired vengeance against a tyrant or oppressor opposed by inclement weather.
44. Obliged to solve a mysterious crime opposed by lack of information.
45. Desired vengeance against one who has damaged good name opposed by duty to loved ones.
46. Obliged to restore health or happiness to a loved one opposed by duty to country.

47. Desired vengeance against one who has caused loss of valuables opposed by enemies.
48. Obliged to risk honor in an effort to undertake a dangerous mission.
49. Desired vengeance against one who has caused injury opposed by lack of influence.
50. Obliged to risk happiness in an effort to brave a storm or cataclysm.
51. Desired vengeance against a rival in love opposed by lack of information.
52. Obliged to restore health or happiness to a loved one opposed by enemies.
53. Desired vengeance against a tyrant or oppressor opposed by a mental weakness.
54. Obliged to solve a mystery or phenomenon opposed by false accusation.
55. Desired vengeance against race, nation or clan opposed by lack of facilities.
56. Obliged to recover lost information or clue opposed by legal procedure.
57. Desired vengeance against the opposite sex opposed by physical weakness.
58. Obliged to risk health in an effort to capture a vicious animal.
59. Desired vengeance against a rival in love opposed by suspicion.
60. Obliged to risk position in an effort to rescue an unfortunate.
61. Desired vengeance against a tyrant or oppressor opposed by lack of influence.
62. Obliged to risk love in an effort to undertake a dangerous mission.
63. Desired vengeance against race, nation or clan opposed by duty to loved oens.
64. Obliged to risk friendship in an effort to expose a vicious ring.
65. Desired vengeance against one who has caused injury opposed

by rivals.

66. Desired vengeance against one who has caused loss of valuables opposed by danger to life.
67. Obliged to restore health or happiness to a loved one opposed by inclement weather.
68. Desired vengeance against a rival in love opposed by duty to loved ones.
69. Obliged to risk friendship in an effort to brave a terrible disease.
70. Desired vengeance against a tyrant or oppressor opposed by distance.
71. Obliged to prevent a terrible injustice opposed by lack of influence.
72. Desired vengeance against race, nation or clan opposed by duty to country.
73. Obliged to prevent a terrible injustice opposed by lack of information.
74. Desired vengeance against a cheater opposed by inclement weather.
75. Obliged to solve a mystery or phenomenon opposed by duty to religion.
76. Desired vengeance against the opposite sex opposed by lack of influence.
77. Obliged to recover lost information or clue opposed by false accusation.
78. Desired vengeance against a rival in love opposed by mental weakness.
79. Obliged to risk friendship in an effort to rescue an unfortunate.
80. Desired vengeance against an insulter opposed by duty to loved ones.
81. Obliged to risk happiness in an effort to brave a terrible disease.

82. Desired vengeance against a tyrant or oppressor opposed by legal procedure.
83. Obliged to solve a mystery or phenomenon opposed by danger to life.
84. Desired vengeance against a law breaker opposed by duty to country.
85. Obliged to recover lost information opposed by lack of influence.
86. Desired vengeance against one who has caused injury opposed by suspicion.
87. Obliged to solve a mystery or phenomenon opposed by lack of information.
88. Desired vengeance against a rival in love opposed by duty to religion.
89. Obliged to risk happiness in an effort to rescue an unfortunate.
90. Desired vengeance aginst an insulter opposed by lack of facilities.
91. Obliged to risk fortune in an effort to brave mental destruction.
92. Relief from prosecution opposed by false accusation.
93. Desired vengeance against one who has caused loss of valuables opposed by lack of information.
94. Obliged to risk love in an effort to brave a maniac or insane person.
95. Desired vengeance against one who has caused injury opposed by lack of facilities.
96. Obliged to risk position in an effort to put down a rebellion.
97. Desired vengeance against one who has damaged good name opposed by enemies.
98. Obliged to risk name in an effort to prove one's strength.
99. Desired vengeance against a rival in love opposed by lack of facilities.
100. Obliged to risk life in an effort to brave a storm or cataclysm.

PROBLEMS
LIST FIVE
(CONTINUED)

101. Desired vengeance against a cheater opposed by physical weakness.
102. Obliged to risk liberty in an effort to brave an air volage.
103. Desired vengeance against an insulter opposed by danger of life.
104. Obliged to risk happiness in an effort to put down a rebellion.
105. Desired vengeance against one who has damaged good name opposed by suspicion.
106. Obliged to restore health or happiness to a loved one opposed by lack of information.
107. Desired vengeance against one who has caused loss of valuables opposed by inclement weather.
108. Obliged to prevent a crime or injury opposed by lack of facilities.
109. Desired vengeance against one who has caused injury opposed by false accusation.
110. Obliged to prevent a catastrophe opposed by lack of influence.
111. Desired vengeance against one who has damaged good name opposed by danger to life.
112. Obliged to solve a mysterious crime opposed by duty to loved ones.
113. Desired vengeance against one who has caused loss of valuables opposed by suspicion.
114. Obliged to risk happiness in an effort to expose a vicious ring.
115. Desired vengeance against an insulter opposed by legal procedure.
116. Obliged to risk fortune in an effort to brave a maniac or insane person.
117. Desired vengeance against one who has caused injury opposed by lack of information.
118. Obliged to risk liberty in an effort to brave a storm or cataclysm.
119. Relief from unjust accusation opposed by suspicion.

PROBLEMS
LIST FIVE
(CONTINUED)

120. Desired vengeance against an insulter opposed by duty to religion.
121. Obliged to risk honor in an effort to escape from imprisonment.
122. Desired vengeance against one who has caused injury opposed by enemies.
123. Obliged to solve a mysterious crime opposed by inclement weather.
124. Desired vengeance against tyrant or oppressor opposed by duty to religion.
125. Obliged to risk friendship in an effort to brave a storm or cataclysm.
126. Desired vengeance against one who has caused loss of valuables opposed by poverty.
127. Obliged to risk position in an effort to expose a vicious ring.
128. Desired vengeance against one who has caused injury opposed by danger to life.
129. Obliged to risk life in an effort to brave a terrible disease.
130. Desired vengeance against one who has damaged good name opposed by poverty.
131. Obliged to risk liberty in an effort to escape from imprisonment.
132. Desired vengeance against insulter opposed by lack of influence.
133. Obliged to risk love in an effort to capture a vicious animal.
134. Desired vengeance against one who has caused injury opposed by distance.
135. Obliged to risk fortune in an effort to capture a vicious animal.
136. Desired vengeance against a law breaker opposed by duty to loved ones.
137. Obliged to risk friendship in an effort to overthrow a monarch.

138. Desired vengeance against an insulter opposed by lack of information.
139. Obliged to risk honor in an effort to brave mental destruction.
140. Desired vengeance against one who has caused injury opposed by friends.
141. Obliged to risk happiness in an effort to overthrow a government.
142. Desired vengeance against a rival in love opposed by lack of influence.
143. Obliged to identify an unknown person opposed by inclement weather.
144. Desired vengeance against a cheater opposed by mental weakness.
145. Relief from unjust accusation opposed by enemies.
146. Obliged to prevent a catastrophe opposed by poverty.
147. Relief from habit opposed by lack of influence.
148. Obliged to prevent a catastrophe opposed by physical weakness.
149. Desired vengeance against a law breaker opposed by legal procedure.
150. Obliged to prevent a crime or injury opposed by false accusation.
151. Obliged to solve a mysterious crime opposed by legal procedure.
152. Obliged to recover lost valuables opposed by duty to loved ones.
153. Desired vengeance against an insulter opposed by mental weakness.
154. Obliged to ris khappiness in an effort to overthrow a monarch.
155. Obliged to solve a mysterious crime opposed by duty to country.
156. Obliged to recover lost information or clue opposed by duty to religion.

157. Obliged to identify an unknown person opposed by lack of information.
158. Desired vengeance against a cheater opposed by duty to country.
159. Obliged to risk position in an effort to destroy a government.
160. Obliged to prevent a crime or injury opposed by physical weakness.
161. Obliged to solve a mystery or phenomenon opposed by lack of influence.
162. Obliged to prevent a catastrophe opposed by inclement weather.
163. Obliged to recover lost information or clue opposed by suspicion.
164. Desired vengeance against an insulter opposed by physical weakness.
165. Obliged to risk love in an effort to escape from imprisonment.
166. Obliged to risk position in an effort to apprehend a vicious criminal.
167. Obliged to prevent a catastrophe opposed by duty to loved ones.
168. Obliged to solve a mysterious crime opposed by lack of facilities.
169. Obliged to prevent a crime or injury opposed by lack of influence.
170. Obliged to identify an unknown person opposed by duty to religion.
171. Obliged to prevent a catastrophe opposed by lack of information.
172. Desired vengeance against an insulter opposed by false accusation.
173. Obliged to risk happiness in an effort to brave an air voyage.
174. Obliged to recover lost valuables opposed by enemies.
175. Desired vengeance against one who has damaged good name

PROBLEMS

opposed by physical weakness.
176. Obliged to risk fortune in an effort to brave a storm or cataclysm.
177. Obliged to risk liberty in an effort to brave a terrible disease.
178. Obliged to prevent a terrible injustice opposed by duty to loved ones.
179. Obliged to solve a mystery or phenomenon opposed by men-
180. Obliged to prevent a catastrophe opposed by duty to country. tal weakness.

PROBLEMS
LIST SIX

1. Relief from oppression opposed by lack of influence.
2. Obliged to risk friendship in an effort to rescue a loved one.
3. Desired vengeance against a tyrant or oppressor opposed by danger to life.
4. Obliged to prevent crime or injury opposed by inclement weather.
5. Obliged to risk happiness in an effort to rescue a loved one.
6. Desired vengeance against a cheater opposed by lack of information.
7. Relief from imprisonment opposed by mental weakness.
8. Desired vengeance against one who has caused loss of valuables opposed by legal procedure.
9. Obliged to restore health or happiness to a loved one opposed by lack of influence.
10. Obliged to risk position in an effort to capture a vicious animal.
11. Obliged to solve a mystery or phenomenon opposed by duty to country.
12. Desired vengeance against one who has damaged good name

opposed by duty to country.

13. Obliged to restore health or happiness to a loved one opposed by physical weakness.
14. Obliged to prevent a catastrophe opposed by false accusation.
15. Obliged to identify an unknown person opposed by duty to loved ones.
16. Obliged to risk happiness in an effort to apprehend a criminal.
17. Obliged to risk name in an effort to escape imprisonment.
18. Obliged to risk liberty in an effort to brave mental destruction.
19. Obliged to prevent a terrible injustice opposed by friends.
20. Obliged to prevent a crime or injury opposed by lack of information.
21. Obliged to identify an unknown person opposed by physical weakness.
22. Obliged to solve a mysterious crime opposed by lack of influence.
23. Obliged to recover lost information or clue opposed by duty to loved ones.
24. Desired vengeance against a law breaker opposed by danger to life.
25. Relief from unjust accusation opposed by mental weakness.
26. Desired vengeance against an insulter opposed by poverty.
27. Obliged to recover a lost person opposed by legal procedure.
28. Obliged to identify an unknown person opposed by mental weakness.
29. Obliged to prevent a crime or injury opposed by duty to loved ones.
30. Obliged to risk friendship in an effort to destroy a government.
31. Obliged to risk name in an effort to brave mental destruction.
32. Obliged to risk liberty in an effort to put down a rebellion.
33. Obliged to solve a mystery or phenomenon opposed by physical weakness.

34. Obliged to prevent a catastrophe opposed by mental weakness.
35. Obliged to identify an unknown person opposed by lack of influence.
36. Desired vengeance against a rival in love opposed by physical weakness.
37. Obliged to risk love in an effort to brave a terrible disease.
38. Obliged to risk life in an effort to brave a maniac or insane person.
39. Obliged to solve a mystery or phenomenon opposed by suspicion.
40. Obliged to prevent a catastrophe opposed by legal procedure.
41. Obliged to recover lost information or clue opposed by lack of facilities.
42. Desired vengeance against one who has damaged good name opposed by inclement weather.
43. Relief from injury opposed by duty to loved ones.
44. Obliged to risk fortune in an effort to overthrow a monarch.
45. Obliged to solve a mystery or phenomenon opposed by duty to loved ones.
46. Desired vengeance against one who has caused loss of valuables opposed by danger to life.
47. Obliged to risk position in an effort to undertake a dangerous mission.
48. Obliged to prevent a crime or injury opposed by duty to religion.
49. Obliged to solve a mysterious crime opposed by poverty .
50. Desired vengeance against a cheater opposed by distance.
51. Obliged to recover lost information or clue opposed by inclement weather.
52. Desired vengeance against one who has damaged good name opposed by false accusation.
53. Obliged to risk liberty in an effort to capture a vicious animal.

54. Obliged to risk fortune in an effort to brave a terrible disease.
55. Obliged to risk love in an effort to prove one's strength.
56. Obliged to risk liberty in an effort to destroy a government.
57. Obliged to recover lost valuables opposed by duty to religion.
58. Desired vengeance against a cheater opposed by friends.
59. Relief from prosecution opposed by lack of facilities.
60. Obliged to risk love in an effort to destroy a government.
61. Obliged to prevent a catastrophe opposed by rivals.
62. Desired vengeance against one who has caused injury opposed by inclement weather.
63. Obliged to risk name in an effort to brave a maniac or insane person.
64. Obliged to risk liberty in an effort to rescue a loved one.
65. Obliged to identify an unknown person opposed by distance.
66. Relief from prosecution opposed by lack of influence.
67. Obliged to risk love in an effort to put down a rebellion.
68. Obliged to risk fortune in an effort to expose a vicious ring.
69. Obliged to risk name in an effort to brave a terrible disease.
70. Obliged to risk life in an effort to brave an air voyage.
71. Obliged to risk honor in an effort to capture a vicious animal.
72. Obliged to risk liberty in an effort to prove one's strength.
73. Desired vengeance against a law breaker opposed by poverty.
74. Relief from prosecution opposed by mental weakness.
75. Desired vengeance against one who has caused loss of valuables opposed by distance.
76. Relief from unjust accusation opposed by poverty.
77. Obliged to risk name in an effort to rescue an unfortunate.
78. Obliged to risk love in an effort to brave deep waters.
79. Obliged to risk fortune in an effort to destroy a government.
80. Obliged to prevent crime or injury opposed by poverty.
81. Obliged to solve a mystery or phenomenon opposed by friends.
82. Desired vengeance against a cheater opposed by rivals.
83. Relief from persecution opposed by duty to religion.

PROBLEMS

84. Obliged to risk name in an effort to brave an air voyage.
85. Obliged to risk liberty in an effort to engage in battle.
86. Relief from oppression opposed by duty to loved ones.
87. Desired vengeance against one who has caused injury opposed by duty to country.
88. Obliged to prevent a crime or injury opposed by mental weakness.
89. Obliged to risk love in an effort to brave mental destruction.
90. Obliged to risk name in an effort to brave a storm or cataclysm.
91. Obliged to risk honor in an effort to brave a terrible disease.
92. Obliged to solve a mystery or phenomenon opposed by poverty.
93. Obliged to prevent a catastrophe opposed by duty to religion.
94. Obliged to solve a mysterious crime opposed by suspicion.
95. Desired vengeance against a law breaker opposed by rivals.
96. Relief from persecution opposed by lack of influence.
97. Obliged to risk name in an effort to expose a vicious ring.
98. Obliged to risk fortune in an effort to apprehend a criminal.
99. Obliged to risk life in an effort to brave mental destruction.
100. Obliged to risk health in an effort to engage in battle.
101. Obliged to risk life in an effort to escape from imprisonment.
102. Obliged to prevent a crime or injury opposed by suspicion.
103. Obliged to solve a mystery or phenomenon opposed by enemies.
104. Obliged to recover lost valuables opposed by physical weakness.
105. Desired vengeance against one who has caused injury opposed by duty to religion.
106. Relief from persecution opposed by physical weakness.
107. Desired vengeance against the opposite sex opposed by duty to religion.
108. Obliged to risk position in an effort to rescue a loved one.

PROBLEMS

109. Obliged to risk life in an effort to brave deep waters.
110. Desired vengeance against an insulter opposed by enemies.
111. Relief from persecution opposed by false accusation.
112. Obliged to risk name in an effort to put down a rebellion.
113. Obliged to identify an unknown person opposed by poverty.
114. Obliged to prevent a catastrophe opposed by suspicion.
115. Desired vengeance against an insulter opposed by rivals.
116. Relief from unjust accusation opposed by duty to country.
117. Obliged to risk friendship in an effort to engage in battle.
118. Obliged to risk name in an effort to brave deep waters.
119. Obliged to risk honor in an effort to rescue an unfortunate.
120. Obliged to solve a mystery or phenomenon opposed by distance.
121. Obliged to prevent a crime or injury opposed by enemies.
122. Desired vengeance against an insulter opposed by distance.
123. Relief from persecution opposed by legal procedure.
124. Obliged to risk fortune in an effort to prove one's strength.
125. Obliged to risk life in an effort to expose a vicious ring.
126. Obliged to prevent a crime or injury opposed by friends.
127. Obliged to recover lost information or clue opposed by physical weakness.
128. Desired vengeance against a tyrant or oppressor opposed by lack of facilities.
129. Obliged to risk friendship in an effort to apprehend a criminal.
130. Obliged to identify an unknown person opposed by legal procedure.
131. Relief from prosecution opposed by mental weakness.
132. Obliged to risk honor in an effort to destroy a government.
133. Desired vengeance against an insulter opposed by duty to country.
134. Obliged to solve a mysterious crime opposed by danger to life.
135. Obliged to risk happiness in an effort to brave deep waters.
136. Obliged to risk life in an effort to destroy a government.

PROBLEMS
LIST SIX
(CONTINUED)

137. Obliged to risk fortune in an effort to undertake a dangerous mission.
138. Desired vengeance against one who has damaged good name opposed by mental weakness.
139. Relief from persecution opposed by danger to life.
140. Obliged to recover lost valuables opposed by lack of information.
141. Obliged to solve a mysterious crime opposed by false accusation.
142. Obliged to risk name in an effort to capture a vicious animal.
143. Obliged to risk position in an effort to prove one's strength.
144. Relief from injury opposed by lack of influence.
145. Desired vengeance against one who has caused loss of valuables opposed by friends.
146. Desired vengeance against the opposite sex opposed by lack of facilities.
147. Obliged to risk happiness in an effort to engage in battle.
148. Relief from habit opposed by physical weakness.
149. Obliged to risk love in an effort to brave an air voyage.
150. Obliged to prevent a terrible inujstice opposed by rivals.
151. Relief from unjust accusation opposed by lack of influence.
152. Obliged to risk name in an effort to destroy a government.
153. Obliged to prevent a catastrophe opposed by enemies.
154. Obliged to risk love in an effort to rescue an unfortunate.
155. Relief from persecution opposed by duty to country.
156. Desired vengeance against one who has caused injury opposed by mental weakness.
157. Obliged to recover a lost person opposed by false accusation.
158. Relief from prosecution opposed by duty to religion.
159. Obliged to risk love in an effort to engage in battle.
160. Obliged to prevent a catastrophe opposed by friends.
161. Relief from habit opposed by lack of facilities.
162. Obliged to risk love in an effort to apprehend a criminal.

163. Desired vengeance against a tyrant or oppressor opposed by false accusation.
164. Obliged to risk position in an effort to engage in battle.
165. Relief from unjust accusation opposed by legal procedure.
166. Obliged to recover lost information or clue opposed by enemies.
167. Desired vengeance against a cheater opposed by suspicion.
168. Obliged to risk name in an effort to rescue a loved one.
169. Relief from injury opposed by lack of facilities.
170. Obliged to risk fortune in an effort to put down a rebellion.
171. Desired vengeance against an insulter opposed by friends.
172. Obliged to prevent a crime or injury opposed by distance.
173. Relief from prosecution opposed by duty to country.
174. Desired vengeance against a law breaker opposed by suspicion.
175. Obliged to risk health in an effort to rescue a loved one.
176. Relief from habit opposed by lack of information.
177. Desired vengeance against one who has damaged a good name opposed by lack of information.
178. Obliged to identify an unknown person opposed by rivals.
179. Obliged to risk life in an effort to rescue a loved one.
180. Desired vengeance against a law breaker opposed by distance.

Obstacles to Love

There are certain magazines which enjoy wide circulations that do not require fiction in which there is a love interest. If you prefer to write a story without the love interest, omit this element.

1. Lover is beloved's political enemy.
2. Duty to profession stands in the way.
3. Kin of beloved has disgraced lover.
4. Lover and beloved are business rivals.
5. Lover and beloved are related by blood.
6. Betrothal of loved one stands in way.

OBSTACLES TO LOVE
(CONTINUED)

7. The match is opposed by a mother.
8. Beloved is infatuated with another.
9. A difference in rank stands in way.
10. Lover is held prisoner.
11. Lover and beloved are cousins.
12. The match is opposed by children.
13. Difference of belief stands in way.
14. Lover does not recognize beloved one.
15. Lover is accused of being deranged.
16. Lover has a past to conceal.
17. Duty to country stands in way.
18. Lover must recover a lost person.
19. Beloved's kin has injured lover.
20. The match is opposed by a grandparent.
21. Lover feels he is not deserving.
22. Beloved one does not recognize lover.
23. Lover has imaginary past to hide.
24. Beloved spurns the love of lover.
25 Pride stands in the way of love.
26. Beloved is supposedly married.
27. Love is not returned by beloved.
28. Duty to religion stands in way.
29. The match is opposed by a guardian.
30. Feud exists between their families.
31. The match is opposed by a father.
32. Lover is her professional rival.
33. Beloved is accused of being deranged.
34. Beloved honor bound to pursue lover.
35. Lover doubts endurance of the beloved.
36. Beloved has forgotten the lover.
37. Lover believes love to be futile.
38. Beloved is in fear of a jealous rival.
39. Lover is ashamed of his family.

OBSTACLES TO LOVE
(CONTINUED)

40. Marriage of beloved stands in way.
41. There is a race barrier between them.
42. Duty to a loved one stands in way.
43. Lover is a member of an enemy clan.
44. The match is opposed by a sister of one.
45. Lover required to recover lost information.
46. Kin of loved one persecuted lover or kin.
47. Lovers are social rivals and one inferior.
48. The loved one is physically incapacitated.
49. Lover doubtful about identity of beloved.
50. Beloved falsely accused of being a pauper.
51. Lover and beloved are brother and sister.
52. There is imaginary inequality in rank.
53. Lover has made a solemn vow not to love.
54. Beloved is not sure that love is returned.
55. Lover falsely accused of being dishonest.
56. The match is opposed by a brother of one.
57. Duty to an unfortunate stands in the way.
58. Kin of loved one once robbed the lover.
59. Beloved has imaginary past to hide.
60. There is a great difference in their ages.
61. Beloved believes love to be futile.
62. Beloved doubts the endurance of the lover.
63. Lover has forgotten the beloved.
64. Lover is honor bound to pursue beloved.
65. The match is opposed by children of one.
66. Lover is pursued by loved one for crime.
67. Beloved falsely accused of being untrue.
68. Lover is ashamed of family of beloved.
69. Beloved does not recognize the lover.
70. Beloved is in fear of a jealous rival.
71. Lover required to prevent a catastrophe.
72. There is a real inequality in education.
73. There is an imaginary race barrier.

OBSTACLES TO LOVE
(CONTINUED)

74. Lover is falsely accused of being a pauper.
75. Beloved feels that she is not deserving.
76. Beloved is ashamed of family of lover.
77. Duty to principle stands in the way.
78. Match is opposed by an uncle or aunt.
79. Convention stands in way of their meeting.
80. Beloved conceals her affection for lover.
81. Lovers are mental rivals and one inferior.
82. Lover is required to solve a mysterious crime.
83. Lover is falsely accused of being untrue.
84. There is an imaginary betrothal of beloved.
85. Beloved is greatly ashamed of her family.
86. Lover required to recover a lost valuable.
87. Lover falsely accused of being mentally unfit.
88. Lover is physically incapacitated.
89. Beloved has taken vows against love.
90. Lovers are business rivals, one inferior.
91. They are separated by great distance.
92. A will stands in the way of the union.
93. Lover has made a solemn vow against love.
94. Lover has sworn vengeance against beloved.
95. Lover accused of deception as to his wealth.
96. Beloved possesses fatal ambition for fame.
97. Lover is required to prevent a crime or injury.
98. There is suspected kinship between the lovers.
99. Lover is possessed with fatal ambition for wealth.
100. Lover is sworn to bring beloved to justice.
101. Lover is required to restore health or happiness.
102. Lovers are professional rivals and one inferior.
103. Beloved falsely accused of being socially unfit.
104. Lover required to identify an unknown person.
105. Lover possesses fatal ambition for fame.
106. Lover falsely accused of committing a crime.
107. The lover and beloved are rival leaders.

OBSTACLES TO LOVE
(CONTINUED)

108. A contract agreement stands in way of love.
109. A misunderstanding is caused by enemies.
110. Professional relationship prohibits union.
111. Lover's country at war with that of beloved.
112. Beloved is sworn to bring lover to justice.
113. A misunderstanding is caused by an accident.
114. Lover is mistaken by the beloved for an enemy.
115. A twin of one of the lovers stands in the way.
116. Beloved falsely accused of being mentally unfit.
117. Lover accused of deception as to his identity.
118. Beloved distraught over threatened loss of name.
119. There is an imaginary inequality in education.
120. Lover is on opposite legal side from beloved.
121. Lover possessed with fatal ambition for power.
122. Beloved imagines she is in love with another.
123. Lover has sworn vengeance against kin of beloved.
124. Kinsman of lover accused of being mentally deranged.
125. Lover falsely accused of being socially unfit.
126. Lover sworn to bring kin of beloved to justice.
127. Beloved falsely accused of being dishonest.
128. There is an imaginary difference in their ages.
129. Beloved distraught over threatened loss of fortune.
130. Beloved accused of deception as to his authority.
131. Lover is possessed with fatal ambition for revenge.
132. Lover is accused of deception as to his position.
133. Beloved distraught over threatened loss of honor.
134. The moral relationship of lovers prohibits union.
135. There is a misunderstanding caused by rivals.
136. Love balked by threatened permanent separation.
137. Lover is known to have broken a promise or pledge.
138. Beloved is pursued by lover for having broken a law.
139. Business relationship of lovers prohibits a union.
140. Lover is accused of deception as to his authority.
141. Lover is required to prevent a terrible injustice.

OBSTACLES TO LOVE
(CONTINUED)

142. Beloved distraught over threatened loss of health.
143. Beloved is falsely accused of committing an offense.
144. Lover is required to solve a mystery or phenomenon.
145. There is a great mental difference between the lovers.
146. An imaginary kinship exists between the lovers.
147. Beloved possesses a fatal ambition for power.
148. Lover accused of deception as to social standing.
149. Social relationship of lovers prohibits a union.
150. There is great physical difference between them.
151. Lover is falsely accused of committing an offense.
152. Beloved possessed with fatal ambition for revenge.
153. Beloved's attention distracted by daring effort to overthrow a tyrant.
154. Kinsman of beloved is possessed with fatal ambition for power.
155. Beloved distraught over threatened loss of liberty.
156. Kinsman of beloved accused of being deranged.
157. Beloved accused of deception in social standing.
158. Kinsman of beloved is possessed with fatal ambition for fame.
159. Beloved's attention distracted by daring effort to stop a rebellion.
160. Beloved falsely accused of committing a crime.
161. Lover accused of deception about his accomplishments.
162. Beloved possessed with fatal ambition for wealth.
163. Beloved's attention is distracted by a daring effort to achieve distinction.
164. Kinsman of beloved is possessed with fatal ambition for revenge.
165. Beloved accused of deception as to his wealth.
166. Kinsman of lover possesses fatal ambition for fame.
167. Beloved accused of deception as to identity.
168. Beloved's attention is distracted by daring effort to save people.
169. Kinsman of beloved is possessed with a fatal ambition for wealth.

OBSTACLES TO LOVE
(CONTINUED)

170. Beloved is accused of deception as to intentions.
171. Great financial difference exists between lovers.
172. Lover is accused of deception about accomplishments.
173. Kinsman of lover is possessed with a fatal ambition for revenge.
174. Beloved's attention is distracted by a daring effort to win battle.
175. Beloved accused of deception as to his position.
176. There is too great social difference between lovers.
177. Lover accused of deception as to his intentions.
178. Kinsman of lover is possessed with a fatal ambition for wealth.
179. Beloved's attention is distracted by a daring effort to instigate a rebellion.
180. Kinsman of lover possesses fatal ambition.

Complications

1. Deception threatens loss of relief.
2. Remorse threatens a sacrifice of fame.
3. Fatal indiscretion threatens loss of love.
4. An illicit love affair threatens loss of advantage to a loved one.
5. Revenge is sought against a kinsman who has committed a crime.
6. There is a child who is not wanted.
7. Deception threatens loss of fame.
8. Remorse threatens a sacrifice of love.
9. Fatal ambition threatens to deprive loved one of achievement.
10. Revenge is sought against an immortal for having brought loss of loved one.
11. Deception threatens loss of health.
12. Remorse threatens a sacrifice of power.
13. Fatal indiscretion threatens loss of fame.

COMPLICATIONS
(CONTINUED)

14. Revenge is sought against an immortal for having brought loss of name.
15. Remorse threatens a sacrifice of advantage by a loved one.
16. Deception threatens loss of love.
17. Romance threatens a sacrifice of power.
18. Fatal indiscretion threatens loss of reward.
19. An illicit love affair or adultery threatens loss of achievement.
20. Fatal indiscretion threatens loss of position to a loved one.
21. Remorse threatens a sacrifice of riches.
22. Deception threatens a loss of power.
23. Fatal indiscretion threatens loss of health.
24. An illicit love affair or adultery threatens loss of reward.
25. Fatal ambition threatens to deprive a loved one of liberty.
26. Remorse threatens a sacrifice of happiness.
27. Deception threatens loss of advantage.
28. Fatal indiscretion threatens loss of power.
29. An illicit love affair threatens loss of relief to a loved one.
30. Fatal indiscretion threatens loss of advantage to a loved one.
31. Deception threatens loss of reward.
32. Remorse threatens a sacrifice of position.
33. There is a rivalry between kinsmen for riches.
34. Fatal ambition threatens loss of achievement to a loved one.
35. An illicit love affair or adultery threatens loss of loved one.
36. Remorse threatens a sacrifice of achievement.
37. Deception threatens loss of riches.
38. Fatal indiscretion threatens loss of relief.
39. Fatal ambition threatens to deprive one of love.
40. Loss of valuable properties threatened by kinsman.
41. There is a rivalry between unequals for achievement.
42. Fatal ambition threatens to deprive one of health.
43. Remorse threatens to result in self-destruction.
44. Fatal indiscretion threatens loss of achievement.
45. Remorse threatens a sacrifice of a loved one.
46. There is a rivalry between unequals for advantage.

47. Fatal ambition threatens to deprive one of power.
48. Remorse threatens a sacrifice of advantage.
49. Fatal indiscretion threatens loss of happiness.
50. There is a rivalry between kinsmen for love.
51. Loss of liberty is threatened by a kinsman.
52. Fatal ambition threatens to deprive one of life.
53. There is a rivalry between unequals for power.
54. Fatal indiscretion threatens loss of liberty.
55. Deception threatens loss of loved one.
56. Mental derangement threatened by a kinsman.
57. Fatal ambition threatens to deprive one of fame.
58. There is a rivalry between kinsmen for reward.
59. Remorse threatens a sacrifice of liberty.
60. Fatal indiscretion threatens loss of position.
61. There is a rivalry between unequals for fame.
62. Fatal ambition threatens to deprive one of revenge.
63. Deception threatens loss of happiness.
64. Fatal indiscretion threatens loss of advantage.
65. There is a rivalry between kinsmen for achievement.
66. Fatal ambition threatens to deprive one of reward.
67. There is a rivalry between kinsmen for advantage.
68. Deception threatens loss of achievement.
69. Superstition stands in the way of relief.
70. There is a rivalry between unequals for riches.
71. Fatal ambition threatens to deprive one of liberty.
72. Deception threatens loss of position.
73. There is a rivalry between kinsmen for power.
74. Fatal ambition threatens to deprive one of advantage.
75. A kinsman threatens to bring humiliation or shame.
76. There is a rivalry between unequals for position.
77. Deception threatens loss of liberty.
78. Superstition threatens loss of desired possession.
79. There is a rivalry between unequals for love.
80. Fatal ambition threatens to deprive one of riches.

COMPLICATIONS
(CONTINUED)

81. Fatal indiscretion threatens loss of riches.
82. There is a rivalry between kinsmen for fame.
83. Remorse threatens a sacrifice of reward.
84. Fatal ambition threatens to deprive one of relief.
85. There is a rivalry between kinsmen for position.
86. Remorse threatens a sacrifice of relief.
87. Fatal ambition threatens to deprive one of position.
88. There is a rivalry between unequals for reward.
89. Remorse threatens to result in commission of crime.
90. Fatal ambition threatens to deprive one of happiness.
91. Physical misfortune or injuries threatened by a kinsman.
92. Fatal ambition threatens to deprive loved one of health.
93. Deception threatens the loss of riches by a loved one.
94. Remorse threatens a sacrifice of fame by a loved one.
95. An illicit love affair or adultery threatens loss of life.
96. Fatal indiscretion threatens loss of health to a loved one.
97. Loss of reputation or good name threatened by a kinsman.
98. Fatal ambition threatens to deprive one of achievement.
99. There is a rivalry between mortal and immortal for power.
100. Revenge is sought against a kinsman who has given insult.
101. Fatal indiscretion threatens loss of revenge to a loved one.
102. An illicit love affair or adultery threatens loss of relief.
103. Remorse threatens a sacrifice of power by a loved one.
104. Fatal ambition threatens to deprive loved one of power.
105. There is a rivalry between mortal and immortal for riches.
106. Deception threatens the loss of health by a loved one.
107. Remorse threatens a sacrifice of reward by a loved one.
108. Fatal indiscretion threatens loss of riches to a loved one.
109. There is a rivalry between mortal and immortal for fame.
110. An illicit love affair or adultery threatens loss of liberty.
111. Fatal ambition threatens to deprive loved one of position.
112. Deception threatens the loss of revenge by a loved one.
113. Fatal indiscretion threatens loss of reward to a loved one.
114. An illicit love affair or adultery threatens loss of love.

COMPLICATIONS
(CONTINUED)

115. There is a rivalry between mortal and immortal for reward.
116. Remorse threatens a sacrifice of happiness by a loved one.
117. Fatal ambition threatens life of loved one.
118. An illicit love affair or adultery threatens loss of power.
119. There is a rivalry between mortal and immortal for love.
120. Deception threatens the loss of advantage by a loved one.
121. Fatal ambition threatens to deprive loved one of fame.
122. Remorse threatens a sacrifice of relief by a loved one.
123. An illicit love affair or adultery threatens loss of fame.
124. There is a rivalry between mortal and immortal for position.
125. Deception threatens loss of achievement by a loved one.
126. Fatal indiscretion threatens loss of love to a loved one.
127. Remorse threatens a sacrifice of revenge by a loved one.
128. An illicit love affair or adultery threatens loss of health.
129. Fatal ambition threatens to deprive loved one of revenge.
130. Revenge is sought against a kinsman who has joined the enemy.
131. An illicit love affair or adultery threatens loss of position.
132. Deception threatens the loss of love by a loved one.
133. Remorse threatens a sacrifice of riches by a loved one.
134. Fatal ambition threatens to deprive loved one of love.
135. There is a rivalry between mortal and immortal for achievement.
136. An illicit love affair threatens loss of happiness to a loved one.
137. Fatal indiscretion threatens loss of fame to a loved one.
138. Deception threatens the loss of happiness to a loved one.
139. Revenge is sought against a kinsman who has deserted a loved one.
140. An illicit love affair or adultery threatens loss of happiness.
141. Fatal ambition threatens to deprive loved one of advantage.
142. Remorse threatens a sacrifice of life to a loved one.
143. An illicit love affair threatens loss of fame to a loved one.
144. Deception threatens loss of life by a loved one.
145. Revenge is sought against an immortal for having brought

COMPLICATIONS
(CONTINUED)

loss of mind.
146. An illicit love affair threatens loss of revenge to a loved one.
147. Remorse threatens a sacrifice of position by a loved one.
148. Fatal ambition threatens to deprive a loved one of happiness.
149. Revenge is sought against a kinsman who has brought misfortune to a loved one.
150. An illicit love affair threatens loss of life to a loved one.
151. Remorse threatens a sacrifice of achievement by a loved one.
152. Deception threatens the loss of position by a loved one.
153. Revenge is sought against an immortal for having brought loss of health.
154. Fatal indiscretion threatens loss of happiness to a loved one.
155. An illicit love affair threatens loss of reward to a loved one.
156. Remorse threatens a sacrifice of liberty by a loved one.
157. Fatal indiscretion threatens loss of relief to a loved one.
158. An illicit love affair threatens loss of health by a loved one.
159. Deception threatens the loss of liberty by a loved one.
160. Revenge is sought against an immortal for having brought loss of liberty.
161. An illicit love affair threatens loss of power to a loved one.
162. Fatal ambition threatens to deprive a loved one of riches.
163. Deception threatens the loss of reward by a loved one.
164. An illicit love affair threatens loss of liberty to a loved one.
165. Revenge is sought against an immortal for having brought loss of happiness.
166. Fatal indiscretion threatens loss of liberty to a loved one.
167. Remorse threatens a sacrifice of love by a loved one.
168. An illicit love affair threatens loss of position to a loved one.
169. There is a rivalry between mortal and immortal for advantage.
170. Fatal ambition threatens to deprive loved one of reward.
171. Deception threatens loss of power by a loved one.
172. An illicit love affair threatens loss of achievement to a loved one.

COMPLICATIONS
(CONTINUED)

173. Revenge is sought against an immortal for having brought loss of life.
174. Fatal indiscretion threatens loss of life to a loved one.
175. An illicit love affair threatens loss of love to a loved one.
176. Deception threatens the loss of fame by a loved one.
177. Remorse threatens sacrifice of health by a loved one.
178. Fatal ambition threatens to deprive loved one of relief.
179. An illicit love affair threatens loss of riches to a loved one.
180. Revenge is sought against an immortal for having brought loss of riches.

Predicaments

1. Sacrifice to passion, habit or mania threatens loss of relief.
2. Madness or mental derangement threatens loss of achievement.
3. An innocent person is accused of having committed a robbery.
4. Kidnapping is threatened to prevent information being given.
5. Advantage is threatened by a revolt against authority.
6. Duty to honor or principle stands in the way of happiness.
7. Sacrifice to passion, habit or mania threatens loss of power.
8. Madness or mental derangement threatens loss of happiness.
9. Abduction is threatened by parties desiring valuable information.
10. An innocent person is accused or suspected of being a coward.
11. Duty to honor or principle stands in the way of advantage.
12. Sacrifice to passion, habit or mania threatens loss of love.
13. Kidnapping is threatened by parties desiring valuable information.
14. Madness or mental derangement endangers life.
15. Sacrifice to passion, habit or mania threatens loss of mind.
16. An innocent person is accused of being a slave to passion.
17. Madness or mental derangement threatens loss of loved one.
18. Abduction is threatened to prevent information being given.
19. Loved one is threatened by a revolt against authority.

PREDICAMENTS
(CONTINUED)

20. An innocent person is accused of having committed a theft.
21. Sacrifice to passion, habit or mania threatens loss of reward.
22. Duty to honor or principle stands in the way of position.
23. Madness or mental derangement threatens loss of advantage.
24. Kidnapping is threatened by parties desiring revenge.
25. Sacrifice to passion, habit or mania threatens loss of advantage.
26. Madness or mental derangement threatens loss of liberty.
27. An innocent person is accused of being a fugitive from justice.
28. Abduction is threatened by parties desiring revenge.
29. Duty to religion stands in way of achievement.
30. An innocent person is accused of being dishonorable.
31. Kidnapping is threatened by ransom seekers.
32. Fortune is threatened by a revolt against authority.
33. Threatened with banishment by legal proceedings.
34. An innocent person is accused of being disloyal.
35. Duty to a loved one stands in the way of reward.
36. Abduction is the result of mistaken identity.
37. Madness or mental derangement threatens loss of position.
38. An innocent person is accused of having committed a murder.
39. Sacrifice to passion, habit or mania threatens loss of loved one.
40. Duty to honor or principle stands in the way of liberty.
41. Madness or mental derangement threatens loss of fortune.
42. An innocent person is accused of being mentally deranged.
43. Sacrifice to passion, habit or mania threatens loss of health.
44. Duty to honor or principle stands in the way of achievement.
45. Madness or mental derangement threatens loss of relief.
46. Threatened with expulsion from an organization.
47. Duty to country stands in the way of fortune.
48. An innocent person is accused of having cheated.
49. Kidnapping is the result of mistaken identity.
50. Position is threatened by revolt against authority.
51. Threatened with expulsion from an institution.
52. Abduction is threatened by ransom seekers.
53. There is a threatened revolt against oppression.

PREDICAMENTS

54. Duty to religion stands in the way of position.
55. An innocent person is accused of being a spy.
56. Health is threatened by revolt against authority.
57. Threatened with banishment by a tyrant ruler.
58. Duty to a loved one stands in the way of liberty.
59. An innocent person is accused of being a deceiver.
60. Life is endangered by revolt against authority.
61. An achievement is threatened by a blackmailer.
62. Duty to country stands in the way of achievement.
63. There is a threatened revolt against authority.
64. Liberty is threatened by revolt against authority.
65. Duty to religion stands in the way of happiness.
66. Sacrifice to passion, habit or mania threatens loss of position.
67. Madness or mental derangement threatens loss of power.
68. Duty to a loved one stands in the way of achievement.
69. Sacrifice to passion, habit or mania threatens loss of riches.
70. Madness or mental derangement threatens loss of reward.
71. Duty to honor or principle stands in the way of fortune.
72. Sacrifice to passion, habit or mania threatens loss of fame.
73. Madness or mental derangement threatens loss of health.
74. Duty to honor or principle stands in the way of power.
75. Reward is threatened by a revolt against authority.
76. Sacrifice to passion, habit or mania endangers life.
77. Duty to honor or principle stands in way of health.
78. Power is threatened by revolt against authority.
79. Madness or mental derangement threatens loss of name.
80. An innocent person is accused of being a liar.
81. Duty to a loved one stands in way of fortune.
82. Name is threatened by a revolt against authority.
83. Madness or mental derangement threatens loss of love.
84. An innocent person is accused of being immoral.
85. Duty to honor or principle stands in way of fame.
86. Madness or mental derangement threatens loss of mind.
87. Duty to a loved one stands in the way of advantage.

PREDICAMENTS
(CONTINUED)

88. Madness or mental derangement threatens loss of fame.
89. Sacrifice to passion, habit or mania threatens loss of name.
90. Life endangered by a strike.
91. There is a threatened mutiny.
92. Name is threatened by a boycott.
93. Mind is threatened by a blackmailer.
94. A race riot is threatened.
95. Abduction threatened by rivals.
96. Name is threatened by a strike.
97. Kidnapping is threatened by rivals.
98. Fame is threatened by a blackmailer.
99. Health is threatened by a race riot.
100. Liberty is threatened by a strike.
101. There is a threatened boycott.
102. Abduction is threatened by enemies.
103. Power is threatened by a strike.
104. Life is endangered by a boycott.
105. Name is threatened by a blackmailer.
106. There is a threatened class war.
107. Kidnapping is threatened by enemies.
108. Fortune is threatened by a strike.
109. Name is threatened by a race riot.
110. Relief is threatened by a blackmailer.
111. Position is threatened by a strike.
112. Power is threatened by a boycott.
113. Life is endangered by a race riot.
114. There is a threatened strike.
115. Power is threatened by a race riot.
116. Health is threatened by a boycott.
117. Love is threatened by a blackmailer.
118. Reward is threatened by a strike.
119. Health is threatened by a blackmailer.
120. There is a threatened religious upheaval.
121. Reward is threatened by a boycott.

PREDICAMENTS
(CONTINUED)

122. Life is endangered by a religious revolt.
123. Life is threatened by a blackmailer.
124. Advantage is threatened by a strike.
125. A loved one is threatened by a boycott.
126. Position is threatened by a race riot.
127. Power is threatened by a blackmailer.
128. Duty to country stands in way of name.
129. Position is threatened by a blackmailer.
130. Liberty is threatened by a boycott.
131. Advantage is threatened by a race riot.
132. Duty to country stands in way of power.
133. Injury is threatened by a blackmailer.
134. Power is threatened by a religious revolt.
135. Duty to country stands in way of health.
136. Duty to religion stands in way of name.
137. Duty to loved one stands in way of fame.
138. Reward is threatened by a blackmailer.
139. Advantage is threatened by a boycott.
140. Duty to country stands in way of love.
141. Health is threatened by a strike.
142. Duty to religion stands in way of reward.
143. Duty to country stands in way of happiness.
144. Fortune is threatened by a religious revolt.
145. Happiness is threatened by a blackmailer.
146. Duty to religion stands in the way of fame.
147. A loved one is threatened by a race riot.
148. Duty to a loved one stands in the way of power.
149. Duty to country stands in the way of liberty.
150. Duty to honor or principle stands in way of love.
151. Duty to religion stands in the way of power.
152. Fortune is threatened by a blackmailer.
153. Sacrifice to passion, habit or mania threatens loss of happiness.
154. Duty to a loved one stands in the way of love.
155. Duty to country stands in the way of position.

156. Duty to religion stands in the way of advantage.
157. Duty to honor or principle stands in way of name.
158. Loved one is threatened by a blackmailer.
159. Position is threatened by a boycott.
160. Duty to country stands in way of fame.
161. Duty to religion stands in way of love.
162. Duty to loved one stands in way of name.
163. Duty to honor or principle stands in way of reward.
164. Sacrifice to passion, habit or mania threatens loss of achievement.
165. Advantage is threatened by a blackmailer.
166. Duty to country stands in way of reward.
167. Duty to a loved one stands in way of position.
168. Duty to religion stands in the way of health.
169. Liberty is threatened by a blackmailer.
170. Duty to country stands in way of advantage.
171. Duty to religion stands in way of fortune.
172. Duty to a loved one stands in way of health.
173. Fortune is threatened by a boycott.
174. Duty to religion stands in the way of liberty.
175. Sacrifice to passion, habit or mania threatens loss of liberty.
176. Fortune is threatened by a race riot.
177. Duty to a loved one stands in the way of happiness.
178. Reward is threatened by a race riot.
179. A loved one is threatened by a strike.
180. Liberty is threatened by a race riot.

Crises

1. Loss of home is threatened.
2. Serious injury is threatened.
3. Disaster is threatened by fire.
4. Loss of power is threatened.

CRISES

5. Learn that a loved one is immoral.
6. Disaster is threatened by epidemic.
7. Life is endangered by a strike.
8. Loss of liberty is threatened.
9. Mental derangement is threatened.
10. Banishment is threatened.
11. Disaster threatened by storm.
12. Loss of fame is threatened.
13. Learn that a loved one is a spy.
14. Loss of health is threatened.
15. Disaster is threatened by revolt.
16. Loss of victory is threatened.
17. Learn that a loved one is a liar.
18. Loss of position is threatened.
19. Disaster is threatened by strike.
20. Loss of reward is threatened.
21. Loss of love is threatened.
22. Disaster is threatened by mutiny.
23. Learn that a loved one is a robber.
24. Loss of use of limbs threatened.
25. Disaster is threatened by boycott.
26. Learn that a loved one is a coward.
27. Loss of fortune is threatened.
28. Serious injury is threatened to loved one.
29. Immediate loss of life is threatened.
30. Loss of happiness is threatened.
31. Disaster is threatened by flood.
32. Loss of honor is threatened.
33. Learn that a loved one is a deceiver.
34. Loss of achievement is threatened.
35. Disaster is threatened by race riot.
36. Loss of honor of a loved one is threatened.
37. Banishment of a loved one is threatened.
38. Disaster is threatened by a religious war.

CRISES

39. Loss of reward of a loved one is threatened.
40. Learn that a loved one is dishonorable.
41. Loss of liberty of a loved one is threatened.
42. About to slay a son who is unrecognized.
43. Loss of home of loved one is threatened.
44. Learn that a loved one is disloyal.
45. Loss of sight, hearing or other senses is threatened.
46. Loss of health of a loved one is threatened.
47. About to slay a father who is unrecognized.
48. Loss of power of a loved one is threatened.
49. Disaster is threatened by mysterious forces.
50. About to slay a mother who is unrecognized.
51. Fortune is threatened by a religious revolt.
52. Loss of victory of a loved one is threatened.
53. Learn that a loved one is a fugitive from justice.
54. Disaster is threatened by enemy creatures.
55. About to slay a brother who is unrecognized.
56. Threatened with banishment by a tyrant ruler.
57. Power is threatened by a religious revolt.
58. About to slay a sister who is unrecognized.
59. Learn that a loved one is a swindler.
60. Disaster is threatened by heat or cold.
61. Insanity threatens loss of happiness.
62. Liberty is threatened by a strike.
63. There is a threatened boycott.
64. Learn that a loved one is a thief.
65. Disaster is threatened by explosion.
66. Insanity threatens loss of life.
67. Power is threatened by a blackmailer.
68. There is a threatened class war.
69. Reward is threatened by strike.
70. Disaster is threatened by a class war.
71. Life endangered by religious revolt.
72. Learn that a loved one is an enemy.

CRISES

73. Insanity threatens loss of loved one.
74. Position is threatened by a strike.
75. Mind is threatened by a blackmailer.
76. Disaster is threatened by earthquake.
77. Learn that a loved one is a murderer.
78. There is a threatened race riot.
79. Insanity threatens loss of fortune.
80. Life is threatened by blackmailer.
81. Fortune is threatened by a strike.
82. Disaster is threatened by drought.
83. There is a threatened religious upheaval.
84. Liberty is threatened by a blackmailer.
85. About to slay a relative who is unrecognized.
86. Loss of fortune of loved one is threatened.
87. A loved one is threatened by a blackmailer.
88. Threatened with expulsion from an institution.
89. Learn that a loved one is mentally deranged.
90. Threatened with banishment by legal proceedings.
91. Mental derangement of loved one is threatened.
92. About to slay a daughter who is unrecognized.
93. Happiness is threatened by a blackmailer.
94. Insanity threatens loss of power.
95. There is a threatened strike.
96. Power is threatened by a strike.
97. Disaster is threatened by epidemic.
98. Love is threatened by a blackmailer.
99. There is a threatened mutiny.
100. Disaster is threatened by the vengeance of a kinsman.
101. Immediate loss of life of a loved one is threatened.
102. About to permit an unrecognized brother to commit suicide.
103. About to be obliged to sacrifice a parent to God or principle.
104. About to permit an unrecognized loved one to be executed.
105. Loss of sight, hearing, or other senses of a loved one is threatened.

CRISES

106. About to permit an unrecognized relative to undertake a fatal mission.
107. About to permit an unrecognized sister to be murdered.
108. About to permit an unrecognized daughter to perish in fire.
109. About to be obliged to sacrifice a brother to God or principle.
110. About to slay a loved one who is unrecognized.
111. Loss of position of a loved one is threatened.
112. Fortune is threatened by a blackmailer.
113. About to permit an unrecognized son to drown.
114. Loss of fame of loved one is threatened.
115. About to permit an unrecognized daughter to commit suicide.
116. About to be obliged to sacrifice a lover to country.
117. About to permit an unrecognized mother to be murdered.
118. About to be obliged to sacrifice a sister to God or principle.
119. About to permit an unrecognized brother to undertake a fatal mission.
120. About to be obliged to sacrifice a sister to country.
121. About to permit an unrecognized father to drown.
122. Loss of use of limbs of a loved one is threatened.
123. About to permit an unrecognized son to starve.
124. About to permit an unrecognized loved one to commit suicide.
125. About to be obliged to sacrifice a child to God or principle.
126. About to permit an unrecognized son to be murdered.
127. Learn that a loved one is a slave to passion or habit.
128. About to permit an unrecognized relative to be executed.
129. About to permit an unrecognized loved one to perish in fire.
130. About to permit an unrecognized daughter to undertake a fatal mission.
131. Loss of achievement of a loved one is threatened.
132. About to permit an unrecognized sister to drown.
133. About to permit an unrecognized mother to be executed.
134. Name is threatened by a blackmailer.
135. About to permit an unrecognized father to be executed.

CRISES

136. About to permit an unrecognized relative to starve.
137. About to be obliged to sacrifice a kinsman to God or principle.
138. About to permit an unrecognized son to perish in fire.
139. About to permit an unrecognized daughter to drown.
140. About to be obliged to sacrifice a child to country.
141. About to permit an unrecognized son to be executed.
142. About to permit an unrecognized mother to commit suicide.
143. About to permit an unrecognized son to undertake a fatal mission.
144. About to be obliged to sacrifice a lover to God or principle.
145. About to permit an unrecognized father to be murdered.
146. About to permit an unrecognized sister to starve.
147. About to be obliged to sacrifice a kinsman to country.
148. About to permit an unrecognized brother to perish in fire.
149. About to permit an unrecognized loved one to undertake a fatal mission.
150. About to permit an unrecognized sister to commit suicide.
151. About to permit an unrecognized father to be murdered.
152. About to permit an unrecognized loved one to drawn.
153. About to permit an unrecognized mother to starve.
154. About to permit an unrecognized daughter to be executed.
155. About to be obliged to blackmail an unrecognized loved one.
156. About to be obliged to sacrifice a brother to country.
157. About to permit an unrecognized sister to undertake a fatal mission.
158. About to permit an unrecognized relative to commit suicide.
159. About to permit an unrecognized sister to perish in fire.
160. About to permit an unrecognized loved one to be murdered.
161. About to permit an unrecognized relative to drown.
162. About to permit an unrecognized sister to be executed.
163. About to permit an unrecognized father to starve.
164. About to be obliged to sacrifice a parent to country.
165. About to permit an unrecognized mother to drown.
166. About to permit an unrecognized father to undertake a fatal mission.

167. About to permit an unrecognized son to commit suicide.
168. About to permit an unrecognized relative to perish in fire.
169. About to permit an unrecognized daughter to be murdered.
170. About to permit an unrecognized brother to drown.
171. About to permit an unrecognized loved one to starve.
172. About to permit an unrecognized brother to be executed.
173. About to permit an unrecognized mother to perish in fire.
174. About to permit an unrecognized father to commit suicide.
175. About to permit an unrecognized brother to be murdered.
176. About to permit an unrecognized mother to undertake a fatal mission.
177. About to permit an unrecognized brother to starve.
178. About to permit an unrecognized father to perish in fire.
179. About to permit an unrecognized daughter to starve.
180. Loss of happiness of a loved one is threatened.

Climaxes or Surprise Twists

1. Wherein the hero makes a sacrifice for religion.
2. Wherein a long-lost one appears or is discovered unexpectedly.
3. Wherein a dog or other animal unexpectedly comes to the rescue.
4. Wherein a pursuing enemy proves to be a loved one in disguise.
5. Wherein it is discovered that a supposedly absent person is present.
6. Wherein the enemy forces are attacked by rivals affording relief to principals.
7. Wherein an officer in pursuit of the hero and knowing him to be innocent allows him to escape.
8. Wherein one is saved by an unrecognized person whom he has befriended in the past.

CLIMAXES OR SURPRISE TWISTS

9. Wherein a witness proves to be mad or deranged.
10. In which the enemy is betrayed by an accomplice.
11. Wherein the enemy discovers that the person he is persecuting is a friend or loved one.
12. Wherein a character feigns dead, hurt or vanquished and then surprises the enemy.
13. Wherein any object which plays a part in the story develops to be other than it was thought to be.
14. Wherein it is discovered that a mistake has been made in the parentage of a character.
15. In which the enemy is frightened by what appears to be a spiritual manifestation, and surrenders.
16. Wherein a child of tender age heretofore unnoticed proves to be an important witness.
17. Wherein the supposedly insane person who has given important evidence is proven sane.
18. Wherein tragic events develop to be nothing but a dream or the creation of a disordered mind.
19. Wherein an apparent miracle of heaven occurs to deliver a character in the story.
20. Wherein the enemy discovers that he is unjustly persecuting the hero and acts accordingly.
21. In which that which appears to be a misfortune is a blessing in disguise.
22. Wherein a chain of tragic events develops to be a story that someone is telling.
23. Wherein a timid girl unexpectedly wades into a fight and comes out victorious.
24. Wherein what appeared to be a tragic situation in the story is in reality a ridiculous mistake.
25. Wherein the enemy discovers that he is persecuting the wrong person, and releases the hero.
26. Wherein a revenge to be perpetrated is so horrible that it enmeshes the enemy.

CLIMAXES OR SURPRISE TWISTS
(CONTINUED)

27. Wherein the enemy in disguise meets the man whom he is impersonating.
28. Wherein the enemy is betrayed by a woman whom he has scorned or abused.
29. Wherein the slain or wounded loved one proves to be in reality the enemy in disguise.
30. Wherein a person who has made a sacrifice of himself is suddenly and unexpectedly delivered.
31. Wherein the enemy is demoralized by an unexpected show of authority.
32. In which it is proven that what has appeared to be the commission of a crime was all a mistake.
33. Wherein it develops that confusion has been caused by the presence of twins or triplets.
34. In which belated evidence comes in after it seems that everything is lost.
35. Wherein the positions of the hero and enemy are suddenly reversed.
36. Wherein the law swoops down on the enemy.
37. Wherein a disaster is prevented by a strike.
38. Wherein the hero makes a sacrifice to religion.
39. Wherein rivals attack the enemy.
40. Wherein the enemy proves to be mad or deranged.
41. Wherein disaster is prevented by a storm.
42. Wherein old enemies swoop down on the enemy.
43. Wherein the hero makes a sacrifice for a loved one.
44. Wherein disaster is prevented by a riot.
45. In which the enemy is led into a trap.
46. Wherein a captor proves to be a friend in disguise.
47. Wherein a disaster is prevented by a flood or fire.
48. Wherein a witness proves to be mad or deranged.
49. In which the enemy is betrayed by an accomplice.
50. Wherein the enemy makes a sacrifice for a loved one.
51. Wherein the hero makes a sacrifice for an unfortunate.

CLIMAXES OR SURPRISE TWISTS
(CONTINUED)

52. Wherein a disaster is prevented by earthquake.
53. Wherein the captor proves to be mad or deranged.
54. Wherein a person or party unwittingly and unexpectedly interrupts matters long enough for the hero to place himself in a position to win over the enemy.
55. Where what appears to be a plot to ruin a character or characters is simply a well-thought-out plan of action to put him or her or them to the supreme test—and they make good.
56. In which the enemy is forgiven by the hero and permitted to go unpunished after having surrendered evidence that clears up the problem.
57. Wherein a chain of mysterious or tragic events proves to be action staged or at the instigation of a clever detective or investigator in order to discover a solution to a crime or problem.
58. Wherein a person who is about to disclose facts that will bring ruin is suddenly killed or dies from natural causes.
59. Wherein it is discovered that some unsuspected character in the story has committed the act with which another is charged.
60. In which the enemy has made a gross miscalculation which causes his plans to miscarry and the hero or heroine is victorious.
61. In which some unexpected or unnoticed thing disclosed the real situation or evidence that clears up everything.
62. In which the enemy attempts to escape, is apprehended and evidence found on his person which clears up everything.
63. Wherein there has been a miscalculation in time or dates which, being discovered at the last minute, saves the day.
64. Wherein some new and powerful weapon is brought into play unexpectedly against the enemy and his accomplices.
65. Wherein a novel method is used to signal for help.
66. Wherein one who has appeared to be a cripple or hunchback or otherwise malformed proves to be a normal person in make-up.

67. Wherein a new invention or scientific discovery is brought into play to clear up a mystery or solve a problem.
68. Wherein a snake, spider or other poisonous small thing, suddenly attacks the enemy and brings him down.
69. Wherein a man who is supposedly physically incapable or a cripple, enters into a fight on the side of the right and comes out victorious.
70. Wherein a judge or other court official at a trial develops to have been a witness or implicated in the case before him.
71. Wherein the actions of a character have all along been misunderstood, and the truth comes out in logical sequence.
72. Wherein enemies are caused to turn against one another with the result that the hero and heroine are absolved.
73. Wherein the enemy is induced to bargain, causing a delay which makes it possible for him to be vanquished.
74. Wherein a disaster is prevented by the results of an entirely different conflict between other persons.
75. Wherein the hero makes a sacrifice for one who has a better right.
76. Wherein an old hag turns out to be a pretty young girl.
77. Wherein a novel and unexpected method is hit upon to effect an escape.
78. Wherein one is saved by an unloved one who loves secretly.
79. Wherein it is discovered that a supposedly dead person is alive.
80. Wherein it develops that the enemy is in reality non-existent.
81. Wherein the enemy is betrayed or defeated by inconsequential evidence.
82. Wherein a tragic situation is shown to be merely a huge joke.
83. Wherein it develops that a person is impersonating himself or herself.
84. Wherein an imprisoned loved one proves to be in reality an enemy in disguise.
85. Wherein a persecutor thought to be a loved one is in reality an enemy in disguise.

CLIMAXES OR SURPRISE TWISTS
(CONTINUED)

86. Wherein a victorious opponent proves to be a friend in disguise.
87. Wherein a vanquished loved one proves to be in reality an enemy in disguise.
88. Wherein a captor proves to be a friend in disguise.
89. Wherein a person who is presumed to be a victim proves to be the victimizer.
90. Wherein an enemy makes a sacrifice for one who has a better right.
91. Wherein a persecutor proves to be a loved one in disguise.
92. In which the enemy is compelled by force to confess or capitulate.
93. In which the identity of a character has been mistaken.
94. Wherein an enemy makes a sacrifice to a memory or sentiment.
95. Wherein a disaster is prevented by a vigilante movement.
96. Wherein an avenger develops to be a partner in crime.
97. Wherein a character in the story appears in disguise.
98. Wherein the hero makes a sacrifice to a memory or sentiment.
99. Wherein the enemy is attacked by mistake by his friends.
100. Wherein hypnotism is used to disclose important facts.
101. Wherein a character unwittingly proves himself a hero.
102. Wherein there has been a miscalculation in time or dates.
103. Wherein an enemy makes a sacrifice for honor or principle.
104. Wherein unexpected assistance arrives from the outside.
105. Wherein a disaster is prevented by rebellion or revolt.
106. Wherein the hero makes a sacrifice for honor or principle.
107. Wherein victory is won by the hero through a mistake on the part of the enemy.
108. Wherein the hero is saved by an unfortunate he has befriended in the past.
109. Wherein the supposed slain loved one proves to be the enemy in disguise.
110. Wherein the hero is permitted to escape by means of a mechanical invention of his own.

CLIMAXES OR SURPRISE TWISTS

111. Wherein the enemy encounters an ambush.
112. Wherein the enemy is frightened by what appears to be a supernatural manifestation, and surrenders.
113. Wherein an act of God brings about the downfall of the enemy.
114. Wherein the enemy falls into a trap he has set for the hero.
115. Wherein the hero is saved by an unknown benefactor.
116. Wherein belated evidence saves the hero after all appears to be lost.
117. Wherein the enemy is betrayed by a person whom he has wronged in the past.
118. Wherein the enemy is defeated through a miscalculation on his part.
119. Wherein the hero is suddenly and unexpectedly delivered by one in the guise of a god.
120. In which a chain of events proves to be staged by a clever detective in order to solve a crime.
121. In which it develops that an ally of the enemy is a friend of the hero.
122. Wherein a near-tragedy proves to be a blessing in disguise.
123. Wherein the actions of the supposed enemy prove to have been misunderstood, and the truth comes out in logical sequence.
124. In which an outside interference interrupts matters long enough for the hero to place himself in a position to conquer the enemy.
125. Wherein one who is on the point of disclosing facts which will bring about ruin to the hero, is killed or dies of natural causes.
126. In which the enemy places himself in a position to incur the enmity of forces aside from the hero and allies, and is therefore overwhelmed.
127. Wherein it is brought out that the enemy is acting under false instructions, and is righted by his superiors.

CLIMAXES OR SURPRISE TWISTS
(CONTINUED)

128. In which it is discovered that a minor character in the plot has committed the act with which the hero is charged.
129. Wherein a character appearing to be a cripple or idiot, proves to be an ally of the hero who assists in his victory.
130. Wherein the hero cleverly bargains with the enemy in order to cause a delay which brings about the defeat of the enemy.
131. Wherein a magistrate of justice proves to be an accomplice of the enemy.
132. Wherein a new discovery in science clears up a mystery or solves a problem.
133. Wherein an opponent who has almost vanquished the hero proves to be a friend in disguise.
134. Wherein a soft spot in the enemy's heart is touched, and he makes a sacrifice to sentiment.
135. Wherein the hero wins the favor of his persecutor by making a partial sacrifice.
136. Wherein startling revelations show the supposed enemy to be a victim of circumstances.
137. In which an ally of the hero proves to be much more clever than was first disclosed.
138. Wherein the principals of the plot are saved by a conflict between minor characters.
139. In which evidence supposedly lost is recovered.
140. In which the enemy, terrorized, falls into an existing natural trap.
141. Wherein the chain of events is disclosed to be a figment of the imagination or a dream.
142. Wherein the captor proves to be in the employ of the hero's parent, who is testing his fortitude.
143. Wherein the enemy is attacked by a wild animal or poisonous snake.
144. In which another character is introduced, bringing unexpected evidence.
145. Wherein it is disclosed that there has been a miscalculation of time that alters circumstances.

CLIMAXES OR SURPRISE TWISTS

146. In which the element of time is introduced, allowing matters to adjust themselves naturally.
147. Wherein the violence of the avenger or enemy brings about a cataclysm which destroys him.
148. Wherein the principal character or hero suddenly and completely changes his tactics and is successful.
149. Wherein the hero magnanimously forgives the enemy and lets him go unpunished.
150. In which the revenge plot of the enemy proves to be a blessing to the hero.
151. Wherein a physical weakling becomes, in the stress of battle, unnaturally strong and comes out victorious.
152. In which drugs or poison bring about the downfall of the enemy.
153. Wherein it develops that the enemy himself is merely a figment of the hero's imagination.
154. Wherein a compromise is worked out between hero and enemy and a minor sacrifice is made.
155. Wherein the enemy is suddenly stricken with fatal illness.
156. Wherein it is disclosed that the enemy is a relative of the hero, and a reconciliation is brought about.
157. Wherein the hero sacrifices his revenge for love of one of the enemy.
158. Wherein an enemy makes a sacrifice for an unfortunate.
159. Wherein one injured in battle proves to be the enemy in disguise.
160. Wherein the supposed enemy proves to be a loved one in disguise.
161. In which the enemy becomes conscious-stricken and confesses.
162. Wherein an unexpected occurrence reverses the position of the enemy and the hero.
163. Wherein an officer of the enemy knows the hero to be innocent and allows him to escape.
164. In which an immortal comes to the rescue of the hero.

165. Wherein an inconsequential act of the hero brings about the downfall of the enemy.
166. Wherein the allies of the enemy set upon him by mistake.
167. Wherein the enemy unwittingly plays into the hands of the hero.
168. Wherein a minor character secures aid for the hero.
169. In which mistaken identity is disclosed, thereby solving the problem.
170. A loved one feigns illness or death in order to secure information necessary for victory.
171. An ally of the enemy is discovered masquerading as a friend of the hero.
172. A chief witness against the hero or principals is found to be insane.
173. Wherein the hero sacrifices himself for one he deems more worthy.
174. In which it is disclosed that what appeared to be a crime is a mistake.
175. Wherein it develops that a character in the story has a dual personality.
176. In which the captor proves to be a friend who is rescuing the hero from a greater catastrophe.
177. Wherein it is proven that a mistake has been made in the parentage of a character.
178. In which a supposedly old man turns out to be young and virile.
179. In which the enemy, masquerading as a friend of the hero, meets the person he impersonates.
180. Wherein the victimizer becomes a victim of his own scheme.

Sample Recording Sheet

GENIE PLOT NO.   DATE   STORY TYPE

RECORDING SHEETS

DIRECTIONS: In the squares below write in numbers supplied by the GENIE, then on the same line write in the corresponding answers or suggestions from the Index Book. Now study the structure carefully *as a whole* and write brief synopsis below—for development into the complete story or to be filed for future reference.

LOCALE		
LOVER		
BELOVED		
PROBLEM		
LOVE OBSTACLE		
COMPLICATION		
PREDICAMENT		
CRISIS		
CLIMAX		

BRIEF SYNOPSIS

BONUS

Who Else Wants to Write Bestsellers That Become Classics?

Get No-Charge Access to
Writing and Publishing Materials
from Our Library Collection

Instant Access - Join Here

Click or type into your browser:

http://livesensical.com/go/writingbooks/

www.ingramcontent.com/pod-product-compliance
Lightning Source LLC
Chambersburg PA
CBHW021955170526
45157CB00003B/1003